"With this powerful, honest exploration, Russ Dean adds a crucial pastoral voice to the theological conversation about divine power. Dean speaks to his congregants, to his past self, and to Christians everywhere who struggle with a world where no one—not even God—seems to be in control. In these pages, we recognize the God who walks by our side through the valley of death and learn to repent of our longing for a divine autocrat."

—DONNA BOWMAN
Professor, Honors College, University of Central Arkansas

"Russ Dean's *The Power of the God Who Can't* is a master class on how to talk and reason about God. The author speaks of 'a theology of reality,' but in view of so much childish theology, this could be called 'grown-up theology.' Dean's book is a refreshing reminder that the last hopeful words have not been said in theology. It brings to mind Isaiah's promise: 'Behold, I am doing a new thing (Isa 43:19 ESV).'"

—DONALD WAYNE VINEY
Professor emeritus of philosophy, Pittsburg State University

"With a pastor's compassion, Russ Dean tackles some of the thorniest problems of Christian faith that have kept many of us up at night, made us retreat into platitudes, or caused us to leave Christian faith entirely. Dean offers us a realistic, faithful, and practical way to be honest with ourselves and others about the God Who Does Everything God Can Do and at the same time to live a faith that embodies God's love, goodness, and creativity."

—SUSAN M. SHAW
Professor of women, gender, and sexuality studies, Oregon State University

"The controlling God some believe in does everything: good and evil. You shouldn't trust this God. The omnipotent God others espouse does far less than what this God could do to stop suffering and evil. That God makes for a lousy parent too: disengaged sometimes and controlling at others. Russ Dean envisions a right-sized God: one who loves 100 percent but never controls. This book presents a winsome vision of the God who does everything loving that God can do."

—THOMAS JAY OORD
Professor of theology, Northwind Theological Seminary

The Power of the God Who Can't

The Power of the God Who Can't

God Always Does Everything God Can Do

RUSS DEAN

Foreword by
GRAHAM B. WALKER JR

RESOURCE *Publications* · Eugene, Oregon

THE POWER OF THE GOD WHO CAN'T
God Always Does Everything God Can Do

Resource Publications
An Imprint of Wipf and Stock Publishers
199 W. 8th Ave., Suite 3
Eugene, OR 97401

www.wipfandstock.com

PAPERBACK ISBN: 978-1-6667-7929-5
HARDCOVER ISBN: 978-1-6667-7930-1
EBOOK ISBN: 978-1-6667-7931-8

VERSION NUMBER 103023

The experience Amy and I enjoyed at the Southern Baptist Theological Seminary in Louisville, Kentucky, was what whoever dreamed up such a seedbed of education surely had in mind, in every way. Our experience nurtured and raised us up, opening our eyes and our souls to a theological world (and to our actual world) that had been beyond our vision—until books and lectures and discussions and friends and meals and professors, like Dr. Frank Tupper, changed us, forever.

We are grateful, and this book is a product of, and is dedicated to, that experience, which has never ended for us.

Frank Tupper made two comments in his course in Systematic Theology that have changed my world. I have shared the pulpit of the Park Road Baptist Church in Charlotte, North Carolina, since 2000 with my wife, Amy Jacks Dean, and my preaching at Park Road might be described as one long, ongoing sermon, expounding and exploring those two statements:

"I believe in God because I believe in Jesus"
and
"God always does everything God can do."

To:
The Southern Seminary Experience (1988–1992)
Frank Tupper
Park Road Baptist Church
Amy Jacks Dean

. . .

Thanks be to God!

Russ Dean, June 26, 2023

If it turns out that there is a God, I don't think that he's evil. But the worst that you can say about him is that basically he's an underachiever.

WOODY ALLEN, THE MOVIE *LOVE AND DEATH*

Contents

Contents

Contents

Contents

Foreword

Graham B. Walker Jr

Prepare to be disrupted. Prepare to be moved off your comfortable center and be reoriented in the way of Jesus! Russ Dean has unplugged the projector that elaborately stages Christianity in the halo of power. Instead, he asks: can we remove the façade and identify an authentic superstructure within Christianity that addresses our true humanity and the vulnerability of our lives together as persons of faith? This cannot happen without returning to the foundational claims that we have made about Jesus and his relationship to God. As he digs deeper, Dean realizes he has no choice, but question our very understanding of God and the world. Dean doesn't travel this journey alone. He invites you into a conversation that began years ago when he was a seminary student in the systematic theology class of professor E. Frank Tupper. Dean remembers a haunting phrase from Tupper that crystalized a way to reimagine his relationship with the divine: "God always does everything God can do."

In the late 1970s when I first met E. Frank Tupper (and later became his Graduate Teaching Fellow), he was one of ninety-four professors on the campus of the Southern Baptist Theological Seminary in Louisville, Kentucky. A native of the Mississippi Delta, he finished his BA at Mississippi College, an MDiv at Southwestern Baptist Theological Seminary in Texas, and the ThD at the Southern Baptist Theological Seminary in Louisville. The twang in his voice reflected his journey and along with the perfunctory sideburns could just as easily have been confused for a country western singer as a Texas revival preacher. Yet, to hear him in the hallways of Southern seminary proved an almost whiplash effect. He processes his thinking and theology "out loud!" one shocked classmate remarked. We were privileged to listen in. Russ Dean was one of those privileged students.

Tupper was a global theologian. His 1961 experience as a Baptist Student Union Summer Missionary in South Korea awakened him to worlds outside of the deep South. Studying with Wolfhart Pannenberg at the University of Munich threw this deeply influenced son of Southern Baptist Christianity into a global catholic reflection on the nature of the church and its place in the world. That world was changing between 1966, when Tupper took his first pastorate in Edmonton, Kentucky, and the intervening years to 1971 when he received his ThD. The Vietnam War was the most obvious catalyst for discontent, but the destructive forces of corporations and the state in relation to the environment, the global push toward neoliberal consumerism which tore down traditional societies wherever it expanded, the failure to adequately address racism, the growing diversity within the United States with the challenges of multiculturalism, and questions of sexuality and of reproductive rights were very much in play. Jean-François Lyotard describes the postmodern condition of this time as one where the "temporary contract" supplants "permanent institutions in the professional, emotional, sexual, cultural, family and international domains, as well as in political affairs."[1]

Tupper was ordained by the Crescent Hill Baptist Church in Louisville, Kentucky, in 1967, where the civil rights activist, John Claypool, was pastor. For Tupper, the deep symbols of southern, white ecclesial life, along with a model of God that views God as a king in absolute control, were crumbling for him. Public institutions, the church, government agencies, schools, liberal arts colleges, and universities, found themselves under severe criticism for failing to recognize or respect the particular cultural identities of citizens. Tupper, like many of his students and colleagues, found himself in the midst of the shifting tectonic plates of the culture. Tupper taught his students and modelled for his colleagues how to adapt, criticize, and evaluate our past for the task of constructive theology within a mosaic of new voices. In an often-cited Tupperian narrative we get a flavor of his awakening to a more feminist voice:

> Back in the mid-1970s I started a Spring theology class with many of the same students that I had had in the Fall, but with some students who were with me for the first time. I went over

1. Lyotard, *The Postmodern Condition*, 66.

the semester requirements, including the option of substituting a major research paper for one of the four tests.

NancyJoy Johnson had written an outstanding paper during the Fall Semester. I commended the quality of her work as a benchmark to the entire class. Then, I specifically asked her if she were doing a research paper again in the Spring. She said, "Yes," and she announced her title: "Beyond God the Father: The Castration of a Concept."

The newcomers to the class were shocked. They had hardly heard of feminist theology. Most of the male students were offended by her straight-forward, surgical language.

The question NancyJoy pursued sits on the front burner of the church—a hot question boiling over with very diverse responses in the church and contemporary theology. The question of the gendered identity of God is now an inescapable question, splattering everywhere.[2]

What Tupper meant when retelling this story to the incoming class of Wake Forest Divinity School is equally relevant in the contemporary church context; how we move from our storied cultures of hierarchically and gendered relationships to full recognition is an urgent matter of ecclesiastical politics. All of these stories of recognition now are drawn into the question of "God" for Tupper. Who is God? For Tupper, nowhere is there a more intimate community and appropriate community to have these courageous conversations than in the local church where we are invited to "grow together as children of God."[3] Here is where Russ Dean continues the legacy of E. Frank Tupper. Tupper's vocational mission was to mentor those who would lead our churches. Nothing made Tupper happier than to see his students find their place in the local church as courageously honest pastors and ministers with deeply informed minds, engaging the hardest questions of the day and with compassion for their congregants. Russ Dean's years of ministry and service within the local church alongside his wife, Amy Jacks Dean, is exactly where and how Tupper envisioned these courageous conversations taking place. In the local church we can learn there is a second trajectory for Jesus:

2. E. Frank Tupper, After-dinner comments, Wake Forest Divinity School Dinner, unpublished manuscript, August 21, 1999 (Winston Salem, NC: Wake Forest University, School of Divinity, 9).

3. In Tupper's *Contemporary Metaphors for the Church*, currently in process, he identifies the church as the family of God whereby the community is committed to each other in mutual growth and maturation.

A Jesus with a legitimate challenge to the conventional religion of his time;

A Jesus with an incredible vision of the coming kingdom of God in which the sick are healed, the poor are cared for, and the outcasts and despised are welcomed to the dinner table;

A Jesus whose radical demonstration of the love of God as love of neighbor, indeed love of enemies;

A Jesus with an unwavering conviction that he must not respond violently against those who were forcing upon him crucifixion.

God Always Does the Most God Can Do[4]

Tupper's doctrine of choice, providence, appears at the convergence and divergence of God's activity in the world and Tupper asked the toughest questions: "where is God?" Where is God in the patriarchy? Where is God in the aftermath of Hiroshima, Nagasaki, and Auschwitz? Where is God in the face of a white racism?

But, who would dare ask these questions in Norton Hall of the Southern Baptist Theological Seminary? And, how could we possibly ask these questions in our local churches? What possible way forward could there be for the "agony of the believer" who could not deny the presence of the divine and the atrocities of history?

In the Fall of 1980, Tupper had returned from Oxford, after having worked extensively on his project: "Providence of God in Christological Perspective." Having the maverick back at the lectern—and the pulpit in Alumni Chapel—reenergized from sabbatical, was highly anticipated among the students. With the passion of an Evangelist and with the precision of a surgeon, Tupper made his scandalous appeal to hear the story of Jesus as the compassion of God with all its humility and challenge to the traditional understanding of the power of God. God's love, compassion, is demonstrated in the crucible of life with all life's attachments and losses. To understand the compassion of God as revealed in Jesus is also to understand that in the particularity of every given historical context of

4. In the Preface of this book Dean notes how *he* remembers Tupper's statement, and how his memory diverges from the recollection of other students, even Tupper himself. As the editor for Tupper's book, *A Scandalous Providence*, I have his handwritten notes, which, along with his book, say "God always does *the most* God can do."

human need, God always does the most God can do, because God's love takes form in conjunction with the realities that constitute the specific human situation.

On many occasions I heard Frank Tupper declare from lecterns to pulpits that "Martin Luther has taught us that a theologian is born by living, nay dying and being damned, not by thinking, reading or speculating." The years from 1981–1983 seemed like the most damnable cry of God's absence as Tupper's wife, Betty J. Wilkins, battled with and died from terminal cancer leaving Frank with two young children. Tupper wrote,

> This I know: Without the story of Jesus, I would not believe in God. Or more probably, the idea of "God" simply would not matter to me. The story of Jesus enables me to envision God as One who genuinely cares for each and all of us. In Jesus, God confronts the Darkness face to face, Incarnate, for our sake. Jesus is the Light to the gentle face of God. The story of Jesus says that God laughs with us in our joys and weeps with us in our sorrows. God strengthens us in the helplessness of our hoping, God stands with us in the uncertainty of our believing, and God waits for us in our yearnings to be loved. Ultimately the lonely companionship of Jesus in the suffering of his passion made my painful journey a sometime story of faith.[5]

Tupper rejected the traditional cliché's that "God, was somehow in control" or that evil and chaos of this life could be absorbed into the "mystery of God." He writes,

> So, Barth erroneously concluded: "As God cooperates with the activity of the creature…*nothing can be done except the will of God.*" Conversely, the priority of God's identity as the *"Abba* Father" **requires the** *reconception of lordship in terms of God's love,* **the** *lordship* **of fatherly and motherly love.** The priority of "sovereignty" over "love" in traditional theology gravely distorts the constitutive identity of God revealed in the story of Jesus: "God is love"….Thus traditional theology had it backwards: The lordship of God is the ruling of the God of love.[6]

Russ Dean boldly, humbly, and compassionately continues the "reconception of God's lordship in terms of God's love" in *The Power of the God Who Can't.* The story of Jesus as the compassion of God *IS* a courageous

---

5. Tupper, *A Scandalous Providence*, 25.

6. Tupper, *A Scandalous Providence*, 48.

and fulfilling way to navigate one's life. It is a confession that comes with risk and joy. If we enter into this story, remember, we must be willing to take seriously and ultimately what this story means for both the very idea of God and the courage to live our lives.

Preface

The theology I share here is my own. This book is not an effort to try to represent Dr. Frank Tupper's theology, but a testimony to my own thinking on this subject, which is largely a result of his influence. While *I* remember "God always does *everything* God can do," a friend remembers, "God always does the *most* God can do." Before he died several years ago, Frank preached and lectured at Park Road Baptist Church. During that weekend we talked about his statement and my theology and this book, and in that conversation he told me he then affirmed, "God always does the most God can do—given the specificity of the context." The theology I have developed may differ from Frank's own understanding in ways, small or large. The purpose of this book is not to compare and contrast my theology and his. I am not attempting to analyze Frank's thought. I believe we agree on the premise at the heart of this theological affirmation, but the impetus for this book is my remembrance of a statement I heard in one of his classes about thirty-five years ago, which led me on a journey that has revolutionized my thinking and practice as a Christian, as well as my teaching and preaching as a pastor. I am indebted to Frank Tupper for inspiring that journey, but all the ideas found in this book are my own. (Don't blame Frank!) I had provided Frank a copy of this manuscript before he died, but he did not get to read it and provide his input. I offer the best of my efforts in this book as a memorial to his influence on my life and thought.

These notes are intended to guide your reading:

The Words

- The trajectory of this book is an exploration of Frank Tupper's comment, as I remember it. The book expounds his statement, one word

xvii

per chapter (God. Always. Does. Everything. God. Can. Do.). In doing so, I hope to invite the reader into the ongoing experiment I have engaged with this concept of God. That experiment was initiated in one theology class many years ago, yet it remains a work in progress.

The Prepositions

- In addition to the Scriptures, I have paired each chapter with a prepositional phrase, indicating a point of relationship with God (God Above Us . . . God Beneath Us . . . God Around Us . . . etc.). Much like the Scriptures used in each chapter title, I devote little time extrapolating specific meaning from these prepositions within each chapter. They serve as a hint of the fullness of God that remains essential in my belief: the mysterious Spirit of presence is the air we breathe. God is the One, *"in [whom] we live and move and have our being"* (Acts 17:28 NRSV). The prepositions are a symbol of my understanding that we are immersed in God, always surrounded by that Presence.

The Scriptures

- The word I explore in each chapter is paired with a prepositional phrase, and also with a text of Scripture. As one raised on the Bible, in the Bible, with the Bible, it was only natural for me to locate my thoughts around that chapter's focus with a word of Scripture. The chapters are not expositions of the Scripture by any means. The Scripture is meant only as an underlying support for the movement of my theology that each chapter relates.

I hope the Scriptures and the prepositions will not distract you. Let them serve only to marinate, maybe to germinate as you read. In the final chapter, p.124, the prepositions come together with the words to form a synopsis of my understanding of the God I have tried to describe in the book. I hope by the time you reach the conclusion, this structure of word + preposition + Scripture will feel less contrived and more essential to the thesis I am seeking to illuminate in the flow of the book.

The Questions

- In my first book, *Finding a New Way Home: The Unlikely Path of a Reluctant Baptist Renegade*, I include a series of questions with each chapter. I provided the questions as prompts for reflection, a way to prime the pump for the words to follow, rather than as add-ons at the conclusion of the chapter. I hope this book might be as useful as my first book for individual reflection and well as for group study. The questions address my hope that you will not simply read my words, but that my exploration of this subject will prompt more words and thoughts and convictions of your own.

The Asides

- An excursus is "an appendix or digression that contains further exposition of some point or topic."[7] One synonym for excursus is "an aside," and I have chosen to call each of a handful of brief essays "An Aside." The topics I've chosen ("Bad Things," "Prayer," "Miracles," "God," and "Power") are all covered in a broader sense in this book, so these pages will all be somewhat redundant—some of these words may be repeated verbatim elsewhere in the book. I have included these asides, however, believing it might be helpful to provide a few more-concise expositions of these broader ideas.

The Sermon

- The final appendix is a sermon delivered at Park Road Baptist Church on May 16, 2021. The murders of George Floyd, Amaud Arbery, and Bethany Taylor, among others, had unleashed protests across the world. Wildfires, floods, and tornadoes had highlighted the immediacy of global climate change. The COVID-19 pandemic had wrought nearly six hundred thousand deaths (at the time the sermon was written) and seemed to be highlighting the long-obvious decline of the church, if not the overarching religious conviction of people across the nation. Is this a turning point, a crossroads of history? Do we need to rethink church? Faith? Our understanding of God altogether? The sermon anticipates a change, offers a hint at a different understanding that I express more fully in the chapters of this book. In a world bent on its own destruction, clinging ever more desperately to power as the answer to all problems, our very conceptualization of God needs a conversion from power to Love.

7. "Excursus."

Suggested Reading

Karen Armstrong, *The Case for God.*
Diana Butler Bass, *Christianity Beyond Religion.*
Rob Bell, *Love Wins.*
————, *What We Talk about When We Talk about God.*
Kate Bowler, *Everything Happens for a Reason: And Other Lies I've Loved.*
Harvey Cox, *The Future of Faith.*
R. Kirby Godsey, *When We Talk about God . . . Let's Be Honest.*
David Ray Griffin, *Evil Revisited: Responses and Reconsiderations.*
Harold Kushner, *When Children Ask about God.*
Stephen Johnson, *Emergence: The Connected Lives of Ants, Brains, Cities, and Software.*
Arthur C. McGill, *Suffering: A Test of Theological Method.*
Thomas Jay Oord, *God Can't: How to Believe in God and Love after Tragedy, Abuse, and Other Evils.*
————, *The Death of Omnipotence and Birth of Amipotence.*
Rabbi Jonathan Sacks, *The Great Partnership.*
John Shelby Spong, *Why Christianity Must Change or Die.*
Leslie Weatherhead, *The Will of God.*
Frank Tupper, *A Scandalous Providence: the Jesus Story of the Compassion of God,* 2nd edition.
Robert Wright, *The Evolution of God.*
————, *Nonzero.*

1

Introduction:
God Always Does Everything God Can Do

"In the beginning God . . ." (Gen 1:1 NRSV)

Language is figurative. It makes an image of God. There is nothing wrong with such imagery as long as we do not let it confuse us into thinking it represents the last word on God. As Saint Thomas Aquinas tells us, we need a lot of images for God. In particular, we need conflicting, incompatible and grotesque ones. The more images we have, says Thomas, the less likely we are to *identify them* with God and the more likely we are to realize that God is the incomprehensible mystery behind all images.

HERBERT MCCABE[1]

---

1. McCabe, *God, Christ, and Us*, 61.

Questions to Prompt Your Reading

Is God omnipotent? What does that mean?

What is the difference between omnipotence and power? Omnipotence and love?

How integrally is the notion of God's omnipotence tied to your understanding of God? Could God be God, if not all-powerful?

Some people say, "Everything happens for a reason." What does this mean? Do you believe this?

How well do we need to be able to give answers about God?

Do you ever feel you need to answer for God?

How different is human love from God's love?

How well does the language of faith, as you hear it in the Bible, in church, in sermons, etc., correspond to what you seeown the world? Are you mostly comfortable with that language or do you often feel you need to justify something? ("Well, what the Bible really *means* is . . .")

Could there be anything more powerful than omnipotence?

God Is Not Omnipotent

God is not omnipotent.

There, I've said it.

I hope the first sentence of this book will not scare you away or offend your spiritual senses, because this book is my attempt to share with you what that admittedly unorthodox declaration means to me and how I have come to be able to say it, even comfortably enough to make it part of the repertoire of my public preaching and teaching. I will try to tell you why the statement "God always does everything God can do" has deepened my faith. And I will try to offer something akin to an old-fashioned testimony, an apologetic for the God in whom I now place my trust, who is, I believe, more credible to a sophisticated twenty-first century world, more capable of touching people's real lives in real ways, and . . . more powerful.

Yes, the God who *can't* is more powerful.

This book is a pastor's reflection, not an academic thesis. These chapters chart the journey that began one day in a classroom in Norton Hall on the campus of the Southern Baptist Theological Seminary, in Louisville, Kentucky. Dr. Frank Tupper, lecturing in Systematic Theology, spoke the words too nonchalantly for a room with a few female students, but mostly filled with conservative "preacher boys." When he said, "God always does everything God can do," and said it so easily—"everything God *can* do?"—a little of the air went out of the room. Someone questioned his theology and his judgment, maybe even the integrity of his faith. A contentious dialogue ensued. It is a dialogue that has never left me.

For many years I wrestled with his words and with Dr. Tupper's impotent God. I wrestled with this God who *can't* until I became a pastor. In that setting, though, given the privilege and responsibility of preaching, speaking honestly to real people who were living real lives and dealing with real struggles, disappointments, challenges, and journeys, so many of the platitudes of faith, which just seem to be part of the southern air we breathe, felt hollow. I simply could not stand in my pulpit and offer trite clichés, feed my people on a diet of the God who *can*, but mostly does *not*. My commitment to speak a realistic word, based on the God I understand through the life of Jesus, and to speak it to real people living real lives, led me back to Dr. Tupper's classroom, and through that pulpit discipline I came to claim his conviction as my own: there are some things God cannot do.

Any friend who could, would.
Any parent who could, would.
Surely a God who could, would, too. Always.

Everything Happens for a Reason?

A teenager in our community was killed in an automobile crash, and a friend of mine offered his speak-easy affirmation: "Well, you know, there's a *reason* for everything." The friend who spoke those words is not particularly religious, but he smiled a knowing smile at his minister friend. He knew that I knew the reason. I wanted to scream, "Yes. There is a reason. The reason is the boy was drunk and driving ninety miles per hour!" Those specific circumstances are the only reason that child did not live to enjoy his high school graduation, though it's not at all the "reason" about which my friend felt so comfortable to evangelize on a baseball field.

I felt that moment was not the time for a long theology lesson from me. Maybe it should have been, because in the aftermath of that teenager's death, parents were grieving, friends were emotionally shattered, a community was trying to come to grips with another senseless tragedy, and in the ethos of this part of the country the word that gets spoken most loudly is "God is in control" (therefore, "there's a reason"). Because moments of tragedy cry out for some wisdom, some comfort, and some healing, much of the popular, conventional wisdom of religion gets conveyed in these moments, and much of it gets shared by people who may not have given much thought to the details and implications of their bold proclamations.

What does "there's a *reason*" truly mean in that situation? God let the boy get drunk? God *wanted* the boy to be inebriated? Was this the *means* of achieving God's plan, this divine reason? Does it mean that God deliberately chose not to stop the car as it careened out of control, bound for the embankment, or that God thought the boy's parents needed to be taught some lesson? ("Maybe we drink too much, and we should have set a better example for our children?") Or did God mean the lesson for the boy's friends? ("You don't know what you have until you lose it?" "Life is short, we better get right with God?") What does "there's a reason" really mean? Do the trite platitudes explain it? "God needed him more than we do"? "It was God's will"? "He's in a better place"?

My intent is not to be crass, and I am not callously unaware of a parent's deep pain in the death of a child. We have experienced such a loss in our family. That accident had nothing to do with alcohol, but that hardly matters. Loss is loss, so I know from our experience the toll such grief exacts on parents and family and friends. I just do not have any idea what "there's a reason for everything" literally means in such a case. The questions I have just asked seem reasonable as a means of trying to truly understand this theology that is so easily preached and too easily absorbed by an unthinking culture.

It is my pastoral conviction that one of two things happen when people learn their theology from such conventional religious wisdom. Some people will inevitably cling to that reason as a means of comfort. It's not just teenagers who act as if they are supposed to be immortal, adults grant them that illusion, so when their lives are cut tragically short it is almost inevitable that the following logic surfaces: if there is a God, then there must be a divine plan or purpose, because this is not supposed to happen. So, there must be a plan. It's just a plan we cannot see.

Any other justification for such a death, dying for no reason or dying only through coincidence or accident or stupidity, would be too painful for some people to admit, so, though it should make no sense to reasonable people that God literally caused or consciously allowed such pain, they cling to the hope that even a senseless death somehow points to a higher reality. A teenager's death becomes a sign that we're not alone. The "Man Upstairs"[2] is watching, pulling the strings, intending even to use pain for some divine reason. It makes some people feel as if we are part of something majestic. Maybe we cling to it for egocentric reasons? Even if all we can feel now is unbearable pain, knowing that this pain is part of God's reason is enough to justify that pain in the eyes of many.

I am not sure what kind of faith this justification creates or emboldens in the people for whom it works. I'm not sure it differs much from superstition. It is a faith that frightens me. In such a faith, human beings just become pawns, helpless, powerless game pieces, just biding our time while God, who dares not be questioned, manipulates the board, every step of the way. We can only hope God manipulates it in our favor. Isn't that what it means? If there's a reason, then everything really is, in one way or another, (pre)determined. And any tragic accident or unthinkable evil becomes fair game for God's purposes. It is hardly unthinkable, then, if that boy's time

---

2. I detest the "Man Upstairs" imagery, but it is all too common and seems to perfectly convey the unfortunate conceptualization of God I am outlining here.

was up, that God actually used an alcohol related accident to "bring him home."

Our only freedom, if this is the way the world really works, is in passively accepting what comes, the good and the bad, as God's will. Everything that happens is in God's specific control, either that which God has actively enacted or passively allowed, and everything, even the worst tragedies, no matter how they occur, become opportunities to see the invisible hand of God made manifest in our very concrete existence.

Regardless of what I think of it, this *is* a narrative that works for many people and, there being a reason for everything, further enlightens the eyes of faith. Believing is seeing,[3] so, once this theological outlook is affirmed, every happening, good and bad, shows more and more clearly the ever-present work of God among us. This kind of logic and faithfulness is comforting and watertight—until it isn't.

And this is the second thing that can happen after such tragedy: faith ceases to offer comfort or quits working at all, and God comes to be seen as hopelessly capricious if not downright cruel. People turn their backs on any hope of finding meaning in this world, at least, from religion. They walk away from a church which has nothing deeper to offer. They say goodbye to the God who could, but just chose not to . . . yet again.

Wrestling with God while living in a community of faith, preaching for people who are enjoying all of life's beautiful joys and its inevitable vicissitudes brought me to a moment of honesty. I cannot live with the kind of faith I have just described, with either of those two outcomes, i.e., being robbed of human freedom or turning from God. What I believe is that this kind of religion is *not* the necessary expression of faith, even for the average church member—and is not a healthy theology for developing a helpful spirituality.

I believe "God always does everything God can do" is a better reflection of the God revealed in Jesus, and I believe proclaiming this God provides more compassionate care and realistic comfort to a congregation. I am not arguing for some kind of sophisticated, intellectualized theology, but one that is accessible to ordinary people, even those who have not been theologically trained. Sometimes things don't happen for a reason, and the church needs to help people grow up with a faith that can accept the

3. The more common expression is "seeing is believing," i.e., when one has seen the hand of God at work in the world, belief is the result. But the opposite is undoubtedly possible as well, and once someone becomes a convinced believer, they suddenly see God in everything.

randomness of life. God isn't in complete control. Thank God. But God is always with us. Thanks be to God!

Is This Really What We Believe?

Years ago, one of the then-most powerful tornados on record touched down in a city in Oklahoma. When the twister finally spun out all its powerful energy, hundreds of homes had been destroyed, millions of dollars of damage had been done to residences and businesses, many lives had been lost. Following this devastating event, a friend of mine sent out praise through an email distribution that God had spared the home and lives of some of his close friends. He called them "prayer warriors," and as the EF5 storm bore down on their neighborhood, they gathered in a closet and began fervently praying. Answering their prayers, after the tornado destroyed every home on their street, God turned the tornado. God let the tornado destroy the next-door neighbor's home but spared their house and their lives. Praise God!

It was more than I could bear. I wrote my friend: "Please tell me you cannot really believe this . . ." A lengthy email exchange transpired, but he never stopped believing that because his friends had prayed, God had miraculously intervened, literally, deliberately, specifically altering the tornado's path. After it destroyed the next-door neighbor's home, God turned it away from the home of his friends. To this day I remain dumbfounded by his convictions. "If God controls the weather so intentionally," I reasoned with him, "why let the storm advance at all? And, why send it into a crowded neighborhood? Why would God allow the storm to take the lives of many of their neighbors, and protect only his friends? Surely, they were not the only ones in the neighborhood who had lifted prayers as the storm's intensity rose? Does God really only hear some prayers? Or, worse, does God hear all prayers, but only answer a few? How do you know what to say, exactly how to pray, to get God to save your house instead of your neighbors'?"

My questions were not answered. Ultimately, I was told, "We just have to trust. We can't question God. We are finite. 'God's ways are not our ways'" (Isa 55:8–9 NRSV). His friends prayed. Their lives and home were saved. God is all-powerful. God obviously answered their prayer.

This may have been a decisive moment in my theological journey. I still remain speechless and chilled by faith in this kind of God, who is the

God so many people worship—and fear! My conviction is that any God who is worthy of our worship, who *could* have saved the friends, *would* have also saved the neighbors.

If a child was playing in the yard and kicked a ball into the street just as a car approached, any parent watching this scene would dash into the yard to prevent the child from being hit by the car. Any parent would do this. No child has ever had to *ask* for this kind of protection. It is what parents do. And if the child had a friend who also followed into the street, no parent who could save both would hesitate to do so. Now, we can imagine a tragic circumstance that might require a split-second decision to be made, the timing allowing only the unthinkable option of saving only one child, but no parent who *could* save both children would choose only to save one. Anyone who knowingly, intentionally failed to do so would rightly be prosecuted for criminal negligence in any court of law.

Is there any reason to evaluate the way God works in this world differently than we would view the actions of such a parent? Yes, we are finite creatures with finite minds, but if we believe God reveals truth to us, surely, we are also capable of discerning justice. It is, then, entirely reasonable to conclude that if God deliberately chose to save one child, and not the other, there is no reason not to view that action as equally criminal to a human who did the same.

There was a time when I would have answered as my friend did, believing we just cannot know the work of God, so we should not ask these questions. But I no longer can live with the idea that God would have us apply the best of our intellect to every discipline of study except theology. It will be essential for the vitality of a twenty-first century church to think as carefully and critically about our theology as we do about any other aspect of our lives. This means being honest about every question of God and laying these questions bare before God.

At this point in the introduction, I need to introduce the idea of love. What really is love? Surely what we call God's love could not be such an entirely different thing from human love, that God's love actually looks like what we would deem criminal conduct when enacted by humans. Could it be? Human parents, because they love their children, could not and would not fail them to the point of letting them suffer and die willfully. If "love never ends" (1 Cor 13:8 NRSV), love in this life would have to be the same as love in the next. There could be no difference in love in temporal existence and love in eternity (earthly versus heavenly love), so God's love

8

cannot be categorically different from our love. This being the case, we cannot justify a God who *could* act, but so often chooses not to act, by claiming God possesses some higher level of divine love.

"God always does everything God can do" is a better reflection of the God revealed in Jesus, and proclaiming this God provides more consistent definitions of love and justice, presents a deity more consonant with a contemporary worldview and offers an approach to the practical disciplines of worship, praise, and prayer that are more integrated with the reality we see in daily experience.

Being Honest

When Amy and I served as associate pastors but were beginning to consider pastoral ministry as a vocation, I had a conversation with a mentor who was a veteran pastor. I was interested in how he dealt with some of the difficult issues of faith with his congregation. How did he preach and teach, and how honest could he be with them? His answer surprised and disappointed me: "You can never be completely honest with people about some things," he said. I still feel the sting of his answer. We cannot be honest.

Why can we not be honest? Is it because church members can't handle it? What can they not handle? Is it the vulnerability of *our* honesty? Or is it the honesty of the answers themselves? Are people of faith not smart enough? Are they unprepared because of a lack of specifically theological training? Are they not asking the same questions, looking at the same complexities that seminary helped us to confront?

I made a commitment that very day that if I ever became a pastor, I would be honest, always honest, with the people I had been called to serve. I made a commitment that day that in preaching and in teaching I would always be honest about what I believe. The questions raised in the stories of Scripture are the questions of all people. They are deep questions. They are hard questions. They are disturbing questions. And the answers they offer (if they offer answers) are not easy answers. The book of Job, for example, is not a text for a fifth grade Sunday school class but for a graduate level philosophy course. What good are our seminaries and our seminary educations if would-be ministers go there to wrestle with life's most complex questions and learn how to confront these issues, but then vow never to take that life-changing experience of encounter and education to the people they serve?

It does not frighten me to tell my people I believe "God always does everything that God can do," and to make it clear I believe this means there are some things that God simply *cannot do*. Through the tragedies that befall real life, this is a truth most will encounter soon enough. The purpose of this book is to help people come to grips with this fact, and to provide a theology that can embrace such reality.

I believe it is imperative to introduce people to the God who will "never leave you or forsake you" (Deut 31:6 NRSV)—even when God *cannot*. If we are unable to provide such a theology, we will abandon the church to the conventional religious wisdom taught in the street, on the radio, at the baseball field. If we do not teach a better theology, people will learn by a kind of cultural osmosis, just breathing the religiously permeated air, which may be especially prevalent in the American South. If we do not teach a bigger understanding of God, the church will continue to fail its people, as well as the world outside its walls.

We who have trained for vocational ministry through graduate level study in biblical languages, church history, philosophy, sociology, counseling, and theology owe it to the church that trained us to bring the best of our knowledge to our pulpits. The material for preaching is often difficult, but that material comes from life itself. Dumbing down our preaching because people sitting in the pews don't have seminary degrees will benefit no one. I believe the church has long suffered from that deficit.

I am grateful for the members of my congregation who have not only been willing to listen, but who have encouraged my wife and me to speak freely, not to shy away from the difficult issues, but to treat them as the adults they are. And to trust them. We believe that in a healthy mix of the ongoing dialogue between pastor and congregation and God (which sermons should foster), the wisdom of Scripture, the tradition of the church, and personal experience, we will be led, together, into a deepening vision of truth.

A Theology of Reality

I have spoken often to my congregation about the need to develop a "theology of reality," by which I mean a theology whose language better conforms to the realities we know in this life. When a child dies a senseless death, rather than pasting a salve over people's open wounds, we need to meet people in the honesty of the questions—even the questions they dare not ask out loud. When they hear "there's a reason," we need to ask, honestly, what possible reason there could be for God to orchestrate such a tragedy. When someone says, "It was God's will," we need to ask, carefully but critically, what kind of God actually wills such tragic, even wicked things. When someone tries to give comfort by saying, "God needed him more than we do," we need to weigh carefully the need of an infinite God against the heartbreaking pain of the very frail and finite parents who are trying to cope. We need to weigh their pain and its potential consequences, very carefully, before we heap this burden of comfort on them.

The conviction I am trying to spell out in this book is that the "God" organized religion and popular culture have given to so many people is not actually God at all. This God is a deity of our own making, a God we have created out of our need for all things to be understandable, controllable. That need derives from our own insecure, selfish need to be in charge, to wield power as self-centered control. How we understand God and talk of God is of vital importance, as Marcus Borg has noted:

> How we think about God matters. It affects the credibility of religion in general and of Christianity in particular. Our concept of God can make God seem real or unreal, just as it can also make God seem remote or near.[4]

Growing up in the world means learning that we are not in control. Maybe growing up in faith means learning God is not in control either. Bad things just happen, to good people and bad people alike, not because God does such things, or even allows them, but because that is simply the way this world works.

This book is an expression of my commitment that we need to teach people to begin thinking of God, living with God, and worshiping God not as some source of brute, supernatural power outside the bounds of this natural world, but as real, honest, "on-earth-as-it-is-in-heaven" love (Matt 6:10 NRSV). We need to teach them to trust that precisely because God is *love*, God always does everything God can do. We need to invite them to understand that such love will always be enough. When we do these things, we will give people a world view that is more in harmony with the actual world they experience in their daily lives. We will give them a theology that will not fail them in life's toughest times.

4. Borg, *God We Never Knew*, 4.

Learning to say and to truly believe God always does everything God can do has given me such a world and such a theology. It has helped me come to grips with reality. It has deepened my faith. It has invited me to accept that the God who *can't* is much more real and much more powerful than any God who could, but so often does not.

God always does everything God can do.

I believe. I hope you will, too.

AN ASIDE: BAD THINGS

"Theodicy" is the academic word: "Defense of God's goodness and omnipotence in view of the existence of evil."[1] This "problem of evil" has been an evil problem since self-consciousness dawned in our evolution. That coming-of-age moment made every "thinking being" into a theologian: Why is this happening? To me? To them? If there is a god? If God is good?[2] God?

The issue has its academic boundaries, but Rabbi Harold Kushner named it in plainly in his bestselling book. Theodicy is *When Bad Things Happen to Good People*, and those bad things are not limited to people. Critics abound who goad God or deny the Divine altogether due to the violence in nature, which Tennyson named "red in tooth and claw."[3] The late novelist, Doris Betts, has one of her characters say it, sardonically: "God knows the sparrows fall, but they keep falling. Ain't creation just one dead bird after another?"[4]

The world is full of pain. "Life sucks, and then you die." My sweet dog killed a squirrel this week, apparently for no reason. Some instinct just riled her up as the cute little guy scampered across the yard. His tooth-pitted carcass is all that's left.

And there it is, all the pain, all the death: proof that there is no God.

Is that it, really? Must suffering and death (all of which is not the result of evil), be an irreconcilable problem? Yes, every living thing is born and

1. "Theodicy."

2. I use "god" and "God" to show the growth of human understanding, from a superstitious notion of a "god" or "the gods" to a more sophisticated affirmation of one God. I am thinking specifically of the monotheistic belief in the God who is "*above all, through all, in all*" (Eph 4:6 NRSV).

3. Tennyson, "In Memoriam A. H. H." line 57.15.

4. Betts, "Learning to Balance," 21.

struggles and dies, but is this really proof there can be no divine presence? Pain and death exist; therefore, a good God is not even a possibility?

I do not understand this *problem* in the problem of evil. Every growing child endures the pain of teething, the bumps and bruises of toddling, the cauldron of adolescent sexuality, the heartbreaks of love. The teenage years are filled with physical challenges, emotional uncertainties, and there is no guarantee that any child, anywhere, will live into a blissful adulthood. Some struggle, and eventual death, is inescapable for us all. In every generation a child dies of some acute illness, a drunken teenager slams a car into a tree. Those funerals are unbearable grief, and all the parents attending know this could have been their child.

Yet . . . parents still exist. All that pain is never cited as proof that parents don't exist! Conscious human beings keep bringing innocent babies into this world of inevitable suffering, death, and pain (and evil?). I do understand that suffering is a gnawing ache. Humans must be concerned, and people of faith must be constantly vigilant, working to alleviate suffering, but pain and death are just realities woven into the fabric of existence.

In her beautiful book, *Ask the Beasts*, Elizabeth A. Johnson writes extensively of death as *intrinsic* to the evolutionary process. "Could the biological world have developed otherwise? . . . The majority of scientists, philosophers, and theologians . . . hold that the correlation of pain and suffering with consciousness seems inevitable."[5]

Suffering *is* a grievous problem, and death is inevitable, but this problem only becomes *evil* if we define God as the ultimate power that always *can*, but usually does not, stop the suffering.

If, on the contrary, God's essence is love, while that would not make the pain go away . . . where is the theological problem?

---

5. Johnson, *Ask the Beasts*, 186.

2

GOD. Always. Does. Everything. God. Can. Do.
(God above Us)

"There is . . . one God and Father of all, who is
above all and through all and in all."
(Eph 4:4–6 NRSV)

Our complex rhetoric about God obscures our ability to speak plainly of God.
We learn to recite lots of language about God. In fact, we often recite more
than we believe. So, a good place to begin our speaking of God may not be with
believing more but with believing less.

R. KIRBY GODSEY[1]

---

1. Godsey, *When We Talk about God*, 59.

Questions to Prompt Your Reading

What is power? What are the different kinds of power?

What would you do if you had more power?

When you think of the beneficial use of power and the abuse of power, which is more prominent in your home? Your culture? Human history?

Does power need to be restrained? Sometimes? Always?

Lord Acton famously said, "Power tends to corrupt and absolute power corrupts absolutely."[2] Is his statement on target? Have you experienced this?

Think of the power of love, and a person who loves you. What can that person do, and not do, because of their love? What are the lengths, and the limits of her/his love? What if that person had magical power to literally control any situation you were in. What kind of relationship would you have with that person?

What does it mean to affirm that God is all-powerful? Can God, literally, do anything? Supernatural things, like suspending the law of gravity? Illogical things, like making a square round?

What is the relationship between God's power and ours? Between God's power and our freedom?

---

2. Ahistrom, "Lord Acton's Famous Remark."

For the Love of Power

When I turned forty, my wife surprised me with a present. Years ago, we stopped giving anniversary gifts, so she explained that this was a special, combination birthday-Christmas-anniversary surprise. She reasoned that if I was going to have a midlife crisis, at the very least she ought to be able to pick it out for me. I have to say, the one she chose was a beauty! I walked out on the sidewalk that cold Christmas morning to find my midlife crisis waiting for me: a beautiful, 1999, red and black Harley Davidson Sportster 1200. We had been riding for a few years and had started joking that when our boys graduated, we were going to give ourselves a Hog to celebrate. Apparently, she couldn't wait. The thing I love about that bike is not its speed. I'm not much of a speedster. It's not the sound, either, though you do get attached to that slow, idling *putunk, putunk, putunk*, and once you're moving, the rumbling thunder is awesome. What I really love about the bike, though, is its power, pure and simple. You can just feel it. When you throttle down on it, the whole machine underneath you seems to be digging into the asphalt beneath. The power is addicting.

Power . . . from the outset we need a clarification of terms. Even in contemplating a God who is not all-powerful, I have found it difficult to refrain from using the word "power" as it pertains to God. God *is* powerful. I still believe God is the greatest power in the world. Yet love-as-power and power-as-force are two very different attributes. Concerning the term "omnipotent," power-as-force or power-as-coercion or power-as-control is assumed, and a literal, unlimited power is implied. If God is omnipotent, God has the power to do literally anything. Anywhere. Anytime. Or not. For any reason God chooses.

Omnipotence suggests the ability to push things around, to make things happen. To be omnipotent is to control at will, to manipulate capriciously, or to possess the *ability* to manipulate, even if restraint is applied. One invariably leaps to those ideas and images when the words power and God are combined.

I believe God *is* all-powerful, but only in the sense that love is the greatest power in the universe—and far too much is at stake to leave it to chance that people will somehow relearn the definition of power and begin to conceive of God's power only as the power of love. If we simply wait on the transformation of that ingrained idea, people will continue to be abused by divine power, as it is expressed among those who hold power. Some will die at the hands of those who believe their empowerment ultimately comes from God. I am thinking of domestic abuse, child abuse, and various forms of state-sanctioned violence from capital punishment to just wars. I am thinking of violence that is ultimately justified by a hierarchical view, with God as the ultimate power at the top of the pyramid.

Furthermore, people will continue to die in "acts of God." This is a terrible expression describing natural disasters, but appropriate to this discussion, as it implies that the best and the worst that can happen, happen because even the weather is God's to control. When these disasters occur, God is invariably either blamed for seeking vengeance on the unrighteous or excused for using natural disaster to accomplish the divine will. (And why would God do such a thing? Well, we don't exactly know why, but we dare not ask, either.)

No, too much is at stake, the death of too many people—maybe even the death of God. We cannot afford to wait any longer. It is past time we changed the words we use to understand God. In the liturgical practice of the congregation my wife and I serve, we no longer refer to God as "the Almighty" in litanies and sermons. I refrain from speaking of God's power as much as is possible. God is love, and anyone who has known true love will understand the kind of power that is imbedded in that experience.

Power Corrupts

The idea that God might not be all-powerful was initially a strange and disturbing thought. "God always does everything God *can* do?" Really, Dr. Tupper? And what exactly is it that God can't do? God is *God*, right? And that is what "God" means, right? God is all-powerful; therefore, God = power. The more I wrestled with this concept, however, the less heretical a non-omnipotent God began to sound. Over time the God who *can't* became more obvious to me, more necessary, more commonsensical, even more biblical.

The world praises power-as-force, in almost every form. We crave it in machines and animals, athletes and politics, in friendships and marriages, in churches, non-profits, and other helping organizations. Human beings, especially out of our weakness, reach for it. In arrogance we cling to power over another to express our supposed superiority. To mask insecurities, born of fear and misunderstanding, power over, even the power-of-hatred, is the tool of choice.

Power is often a synonym of abuse, because it so intrinsically implies a situation of inequality, a relationship of dominance and submission, the failure of one party to acknowledge the identity, character, or rights of the other. This is true of individuals as well as groups and systems, small and great. When we think of governments or military regimes, the word powerful often connotes a range of negative emotions, from corruption, to oppression, to manifest evil. Think of Caesar's Rome and Hitler's Germany, of Pinochet's Chile and Saddam's Iraq. I sometimes hear people applaud the restraint of the United States' use of power-as-force. Whether or not one agrees with that evaluation of the world's so-called most powerful nation, the statement itself clarifies the point, namely, that power must be restrained because there is an inherent, destructive seed at its heart.

One might argue that power, in and of itself, is not destructive, that it can be used for good or ill. It's like that old argument about money: wait now, the Bible never says *money* is evil, it says "the *love* of money is the root of all evil!" (1 Tim 6:10 NRSV). This is a specious argument, and one that is always made a bit too defensively to ring true. Did Jesus ever say anything about money that doesn't cast a negative light on it? Of course money is not evil, in and of itself, but what Jesus clearly understood is that it is nearly impossible to possess money, even a little bit of it, without it possessing you. Likewise, one might attempt to defend power as a neutral quality, in theory, but the universal inevitability of power-as-abuse belies that argument.

To evaluate this idea, we might test a different word, a word with opposite characteristics. We might ask if the same argument could be made of love, in the opposite direction. Some might argue that power itself is not a bad thing, but would anyone ever have to argue that love really is a *good* thing? Isn't that clear on its face? Any emotion or characteristic or relationship that is abusive or destructive could never be called love. The point is: the word love is as clear in its connotations of goodness, as power is in its associations with abuse.

How, then, might God be all-powerful if "God is love" (1 John 4:8 NRSV)? Do the qualities of power and love not imply tension, contradiction, maybe even ideas that are diametric opposites? Love forsakes power-as-force, always. Love plays by different rules, completely. Love reframes the argument, resets the stage, reenvisions . . . everything!

Power "lords over" (Matt 20:25 NRSV); love submits. Power is jealous; "love is kind" (1 Cor 13:4 NRSV). Power dominates, protects self at the expense of the other; "love lays down its life for its friends" (John 15:13

NRSV). Power seeks the equilibrium of the status quo; love is revolutionary, "lifting the lowly, humbling the mighty" (Luke 1:52 NRSV). Power causes suffering; love accepts suffering and transforms it into joy. Power is manipulative; love is creative.

Lord Acton famously said, "Power tends to corrupt and absolute power corrupts absolutely."[3] Has it ever not been so? And if absolute power tends to corrupt absolutely, could God, who is the Absolute, really be *power*? I believe an understanding of God as absolute power has thoroughly corrupted our concept of God, and concern for what that means, in practical terms, has led me to the unconventional notion of God beyond power. That idea is now the center of my theology.

In *The Great Partnership*, Rabbi Lord Jonathan Sacks, who has been called "one of the most admired religious thinkers of our time,"[4] defends religion and science as twin disciplines, compatible and equally important in developing advanced and meaningful societies. In his defense of religion, however, Sacks is not blind to the egregious failures of religion throughout history, and he critiques religion in the twenty-first century as tending to "repressive, rights-denying, even brutal regimes." What is the cause of such misguided religion, according to Sacks?

> They break the rule of Abrahamic faith . . . that religion should never wield *power*. Religion . . . is a principled opposition to the will to power. Faith is about the forms of gracious coexistence that abjure the use of power.[5]

While Sacks's thesis does not critique a theology of omnipotence, per se, his insight invites us to ask this: If any religious tradition has, unfortunately, given legitimacy to the concept of omnipotence, how could that tradition offer any meaningful critique of the abuse of power itself? If God is omnipotent power, as any religion that "breaks the rule of Abrahamic faith" claims, how could that religion avoid wielding power? And why should it? Shouldn't the proponents of religion and the institutions of religion not seek to embody the very values and traits, the characteristics of the God who inspires that religion?

3. Ahlstrom, "Lord Acton's Famous Remark."

4. This accolade graces the back cover of this book.

5. Sacks, *Great Partnership*, 104 (emphasis added). I accept Sacks's thesis, that, at least in its ideal expression, faith abjures power, yet it is worth noting that Abraham himself was a man of wealth and power, an owner of slaves, and that his power was attributed to God.

The word "omnipotent" ought to be troublesome from the start. To say God is all-powerful is to imply that God is absolute power-as-force. It is to say that power-as-control or power-as-coercion is God's nature, the very essence of what God is. This should be troubling in all that this implies for those who seek to know God and to follow God. If God is love, then isn't power-as-force something God, by the very definition of love, cannot be?

In defending omnipotence, it could be argued that God alone could possess all power, because only God could rightly use power. This is a sufficient argument, but not a necessary one. Once humans defined God as all-powerful *and* all-loving, it became necessary to defend this definition of God's nature, even if doing so was illogical, even contradictory. Long, wearying arguments have been made defending the paradox of God's power vis-à-vis God's love, but why are such confounding arguments even necessary? I believe they are not.

God's Will

Leslie Weatherhead's book *The Will of God* is a wonderful treatment of the troublesome phrase "the will of God."[6] I have often recommended this book, which was written out of a series of sermons delivered to a congregation in London as the bombs of World War II were raining from the sky. All theology should be developed as Weatherhead's was—in the crucible of life, not a vacuum of ivory tower speculation. Out of that crucible of experience, Weatherhead writes of God's "intentional will," God's "circumstantial will," and God's "ultimate will." If God literally has the power to control everything, but we don't want to hold God accountable for hardship and disease and death, then we must construct a system for explaining why bad things happen to good people.[7]

Weatherhead does this admirably, suggesting that God's "intentional will" is what God actually *intends* to happen; this intention is always for the good. But God, having limited God's own omnipotence, will not intervene at every moment, thus allowing a "circumstantial will" to rule day-to-day affairs. Finally, because Christians believe "in all things, God is working to bring about good" (Rom 8:28 NRSV), Weatherhead defines God's "ultimate will" as God using life's inevitable bad circumstances for a better purpose.

6. Weatherhead, *Will of God.*

7. I have taken this phrase from the book title by Harold Kushner, *Why Bad Things Happen to Good People.*

Think of the biblical Jacob. His brothers try to kill him only to discover, years later, that he is second in command of all Egypt. They begin to fear for their lives, but Joseph says, "What you intended for evil, God intended for good." (Gen 50:20 NRSV).

Weatherhead's book presents a useful strategy to which I continue to recommend when someone is beginning to ask the troubling question of love and power (love versus power), but it is a strategy designed to release God from the logical consequences of a theology that unnecessarily defines God as all-powerful from the start. His carefully constructed argument provides an excellent example of the wearying, contradictory logic that becomes necessary in order to harmonize the incompatibility of all-power and love.

> The omnipotence of God, you perceive, does not mean that by a sheer exhibition of [God's] superior might ["brute strength"] God gets [God's] own way. If that were the case, human freedom would be an illusion and human moral development would be made impossible.[8]

While admirable and necessary for his theological construction, this paragraph is nonsensical. Either God is omnipotent, or God is not. It cannot be both ways. Weatherhead's commitment to orthodoxy requires that he defend omnipotence, so he must redefine the word to mean something other than all-powerful. In this (il)logic, omnipotence becomes all-powerful—only as we *perceive* it—yet, by definition, omnipotent means all-powerful whether we perceive it or not.

My conviction is that we should just come clean and say what we mean and mean what we say about God. We should not need to harmonize the cognitive dissonance between our theology and our experience. We need to learn to speak clearly about what we have experienced, not just recite the old dogmas that have become part of the vernacular. If we could learn to do so, which would require some unlearning, we might truly believe what we have experienced and experience what we have believed.

If God is love, why not simply affirm this?

Dispensing with the implicitly troubling notion of God as all-powerful would free us from the necessity of employing crafty but illogical theological gymnastics to defend God. In the process, it would free humanity

8. Weatherhead, *Will of God*, 34. "At-one-ment" is an intentional parsing of the word atonement.

to pursue that "higher way" (1 Cor 12:31 NRSV) of love, which, alone, can transform us as individuals and as a collective community.

Looking for a Biblical Justification

Hidden within the clever rationalization and necessary justification of God's omnipotence is the human desire for power. Omnipotence is the projection of a human desire, and a sinful one at that, onto the nature of God. There is undoubtedly a developmental origin. As humans developed a self-consciousness alongside a developing God-consciousness, the harsh necessity of survival suggested power-as-force be projected into the supreme quality of a Supreme Being. (If power is "God," then God is power.)

Is there also a biblical origin to the concept of omnipotence? Instinctively, we who were raised in the Good Book might say yes. "God said, 'Let there be . . .'" (Gen 1:3 NRSV). Isn't creating the world enough to prove God's omnipotence? God parted the Red Sea for Moses (Exod 14). God hurled stones on the Amorites, killing many in order to protect the Israelites (Josh 10:11).

Do these, and many other examples that could be given, however, justify a definition and belief in God's absolute omnipotence? We must consider that the context of these Old Testament proof texts is a polytheistic culture. Monotheism was slow to develop, and it is likely that many of these ancient stories were told in order to proclaim the victory of Israel's god, whom they called Yahweh, the one God, over the gods of a warring nation.

The prohibition against idol making is a frequent concern of the Old Testament and is closely related to the first commandment, "you shall have no other Gods" (Exod 20:3 NRSV). John Holbert says that in the biblical chronology only with the book of Ezra, however, is there finally silence concerning idolatry. This suggests that it took more than a thousand years for monotheism to fully take root in the Jewish mind. Holbert also says that the form of this commandment suggests "with certainty that Israel did not avoid image making or the worship of images."[9]

This long history of polytheism indicates Israel's struggle to fully claim the affirmation "the Lord our God, the Lord is *one*" (Deut 6:4 NRSV; emphasis added). Given that struggle, the power presented in Old Testament depictions of Israel's God might be understood better as a relative power (power over other gods) than absolute, all-encompassing power. In that

9. Holbert, *Ten Commandments*, 26.

context, proclaiming the all-powerfulness of God rings with a bit of tribalism, like claiming, "My god's bigger than your god."

Merriam-Webster states that the "first known use" of the English noun "omnipotent" was in the year 1600, having been used as an adjective since the fourteenth century. "Although *omnipotent* is used in general contexts to mean 'all-powerful' (as in 'an omnipotent warlord'), its original applications in English referred specifically to the power held by an almighty God."[10] It is worth considering which came first, however. Did the notion of an all-powerful God give legitimacy to kings and structures of hierarchy, or did power hungry warlords, claiming total control over their subjects, promote the idea of omnipotence for their own, selfish purposes?

In the introduction to the Authorized Version of the Bible, better known as the King James Version, we read,

> To the most high and mightie Prince, James by the grace of God King of Great Britaine, France and Ireland, Defender of the Faith, &c. The translators of The Bible, wish Grace, Mercie, and Peace, through Jesus Christ our Lord. Great and manifold were the blessings (most dread Soveraigne) which Almighty GOD, the Father of all Mercies, bestowed upon us the people of ENGLAND.[11]

From this introduction, the importance that power of hierarchy exhibited in that English society is immediately obvious. The most high James enacted his omnipotent power across the land by virtue of the "divine right of kings," the belief that all earthly power derived from God's power. Kings were quick to remind their subjects that their power was unquestioned, having been ordained of God. Did an Almighty God give power to the kings of the land, or did *omnipotent* kings justify their own absolute power through the creation of a theology of omnipotence?

The Hebrew word translated "almighty" is *shaddai*, possibly derived from *shaddad*, "to be burly, powerful, impregnable."[12] Other commentators, however, note the association with the Hebrew, *shad*, which means "breasts." The internet is rife with commentaries explaining the origin of the "all-sufficient" God, such as, "the name might derive from the contraction of *sha* ('who') and *dai* ('enough') to indicate God's complete sufficiency to nurture the fledgling nation into fruitfulness."[13] There is a world of differ-

10. "Omnipotent."
11. KJV, iii.
12. Strong, *Strong's Exhaustive Concordance*, 113.
13. Parsons, "Hebrew Name of God," §7.

ence in translation, interpretation, and implication between an overpowering, destroying God (*El Shaddai*), however, and a mothering, nurturing God by the same name (*El Shaddai*). Why, then, did "almighty" become the preferable treatment of *shaddai* in English translations, beginning in the sixteenth and seventeenth centuries? In the King James Version of the Bible, *shaddai* is translated "almighty" all fifty-seven times it appears in the text.

Similarly, in the New Testament, the Greek word *pantocrator* is translated "the ruler of all things," yet we find a similar question embedded within the definition and translation of this word. Namely, is "ruler of all things" equivalent to "omnipotent"? In *Strong's Exhaustive Concordance of the Bible* the word is defined as "the *all-ruling*, i.e., *God* (as absolute and universal *sovereign*):—Almighty, Omnipotent."[14] Yet, the root word *kratos* means "vigor." Vigor may include power or force, but this is not a necessary connotation.

A vigorous criminal defense can be argued in court without resulting in an acquittal. Many vigorous athletic challenges have been made without dethroning a champion. Vigor is an admirable and inspirational trait. It doesn't necessarily make one invincible. Is God's greatness or vigor only to be defined by unlimited power-as-force? Perhaps the fear invoked by and the violence often perpetrated in the name of an overpowering Almighty even overshadows God's real greatness.

In the extensive and definitive nine-volume *Theological Dictionary of the New Testament*, the Greek word *pantocrator* is defined as "the almighty," "the ruler of all things," yet the entry states, "The reference is not so much to God's activity in creation as to [God's] supremacy over all things." A footnote adds, "Not '*power over* all things.'"[15] In the dictionary's entry for *dunamis* (Greek for "power"), we also read, "[God's] power is not caprice; it is the expression of [God's] will and is thus determined by the content of [God's] will, which consists in righteousness. . . .The power of God constitutes the inner energy of holiness and gives it the character of the inaccessible and transcendent."[16]

What does the Bible really say? In *our* need for God to be all-powerful, justifying our love of power, have we taken a word with theological significance, a word with deep and diverse implications, a claim that in all

14. Strong, *Strong's Exhaustive Concordance*, 54.

15. Kittel, *Theological Dictionary*, 3.914–15 (emphasis added).

16. Kittel, *Theological Dictionary*, 2.293.

things God *is* supreme—supreme in wisdom, in importance, in vitality, in creativity, supreme in love, etc.—and forced that word into a mold of power-as-control, alone?

The discipline of translation is difficult and fascinating, and its importance cannot be underestimated. The all-important question I am asking is how will we translate the language of God, and how will we "translate God," personally and for our world?[17]

The Image of the Invisible God

As the church began to sort out its understanding of Jesus, competing theologies and Christologies were abundant and diverse. The confrontation that settled the issue, defining the orthodox position, took place between two bishops named Arius and Athanasius. The God Athanasius said had been revealed in Jesus of Nazareth was hardly the High God Arius defended. God, revealed with a human face, did not resemble absolute power but shared the divine nature in a coequal triune community and participated in the weakness of humanity, condescending to "become flesh" (John 1:14 NRSV) even in humility, "submitting to death on a cross" (Phil 2:8 NRSV). Could this really be an all-powerful deity Athanasius was describing?[18]

The uniquely Christian idea of divine incarnation should make this point crystal clear. God's full participation in our very humanity is anathema to the Jews and Muslims who, otherwise, share the monotheism of Christianity. That the Almighty should submit to death, through God's incarnational representative, Jesus, is a blasphemous heresy.

A few years ago, I hosted a meeting of a group of men in the church that we called the Iotas, because "nothing is too small to be a big deal." The Iotas was an unorthodox gathering at Sir Edmund Halley's English Pub to talk theology. One night we had gathered to listen to a friend of mine who was then the rabbi in Charlotte's Conservative Jewish temple. My friend had enlightened us with some of the finer points of Jewish theology when someone asked a question about the feminine aspect of God. As he

17. In his book, *The Death of Omnipotence and the Birth of Amipotence*, Thomas Jay Oord provides a fascinating, detailed examination of the concept of omnipotence in the Bible, addressing "biblical words and phrases pertaining to divine power: *shaddai, sabaoth*, and *pantokrator*." Oord concludes, "Each is wrongly translated 'almighty.'" See his chapter entitled "Not Born of Scripture," 11.

18. For a helpful, concise summary of the conversation between Arius and Athanasius, see McGill, *Suffering*.

answered, talking about different aspects of God's nature, the distant and the near, the protecting and the nurturing, I heard language virtually identical to the language Christians use to speak of a Trinitarian God: one God in three experiences. I stifled my grin long enough to interject, "Oh—just like the Trinity!" There were a few smirks around the table, but my friend nearly came out of his seat. There was nothing funny about my Baptist humor, and he let me know, nearly spitting across the table, "It's *not at all* like the Trinity!" The blasphemy of Trinitarian theology, for Jews, is the suggestion that God could *in any way* be revealed in a human life. Any human life. God is *God*, and humans are, well, just human.

Another friend of mine who is the Imam at one of Charlotte's mosques defined the Arabic word *tawheed* as "pure, absolutely, transcendentally One—that which is truly pure and flawless." In Islamic thought it is inconceivable that God could ever be part of the finite, flawed, ever-changing, corruptible universe. Muslims could never affirm that "God was in Christ" (2 Cor 5:19 NRSV) or in any other person. Incarnation is a scandalous theology.

While many of the religious of the world will scoff at the notion that God is *not* all-powerful, the incarnational theology at the heart of Christianity should invite Christians to reconsider. If Jesus is the "image of the invisible God" (Col 1:15 NRSV), his ministry, his teaching, his life, and his death demand that Christians reconsider our theological position.

To paraphrase the feminist critique, if God is "power" then "power" is God.[19] Our image of God, the way we are taught to conceive of God, in any practical sense *becomes* God. Given the way language functions in our minds, making this connection is nearly inevitable and impossible to avoid. Herein lies the danger. Charles Hartshorne, aware of such danger, writes of this in his book, *The Divine Relativity*:

> Thus "brute power" is an indirect relation, never a direct one. But it is none-the-less practically efficacious, for good or ill, and has to be reckoned with. The one thing we need not and ought not to do is—to worship it![20]

But worship power-as-control we have, and, as a result, an all-powerful God has given at least indirect license to an inconceivable assortment of abuses and brutalities. Reframing God as love, not power, would not

19. Mary Daly says, "If God is male, the male is God." Daly, *Beyond God the Father*, 40.

20. Hartshorne, *Divine Relativity*, 155.

end human evil and the atrocities we inflict upon each other, but surely no one could imagine a husband abusing his wife in the name of a God of love. Men do not fly loaded passenger airplanes into occupied New York City skyscrapers to appease a God of love. Violence in our world would not disappear, but one can only imagine that it would have to decrease if humans were not able give a divine justification for such violence. If sacred Scriptures were not read only in such a way as to legitimate a deity of force and control and coercion, surely a change could be measured in human behavior.

Religion is the most pervasive, lasting institution the world has ever known. Religion holds a persuasive influence over its adherents, promoting its ideas and ideals as a guide for the thoughts and attitudes that influence the actions of true believers. The time is long overdue for religions to outgrow their tribal origins, the fear-based theologies that justify a survivalist mentality, i.e., "only the strong will survive." Religion may have protected ancient people by providing that justification, i.e. the use of force in warfare, but the technological advance of modernity and the weapons available to us make that mentality, and the God behind it, a sure recipe for mutually assured destruction (sheer MADness). Power-as-force may have brought us to the dance, but only love-as-power will be able to take us home. The faith Jesus proclaimed so very long ago strongly contradicts thinking of God as omnipotent coercion and ultimate control. Isn't it time we began to practice what he preached?

Less Alpha, More Omega

In *Adventures of Ideas* Alfred North Whitehead says, "The worst of unqualified omnipotence is that it is accompanied by responsibility for every detail of every happening."[21] This is another area in which many Christians do not follow the logical argument, the necessary conclusion of their theology. Especially if one affirms the traditional expression of God's *creatio ex nihilo* (creation out of nothing), could there be any other explanation for the existence of evil than that it is ultimately God's responsibility?

According to the traditional reading, there was nothing, and then there was something. In fact, with God's spoken word, there was everything: life, and with it the existence of evil and the freedom to choose evil over good. But, if God had created absolutely everything, from absolutely

21. Whitehead, *Adventures of Ideas*, 217.

nothing, then how could there be *evil*? Where did evil come from? And what would freedom mean, that being the case? Could there be any true freedom? Who gave Adam and Eve the freedom to choose evil? And . . . why!?

The common response to these questions is to retreat in safety: "The Bible says . . . and we can't know . . . so we should not ask those questions to begin with." But this will not suffice for Christians who truly seek to love God with all their *minds* (Mark 12:30 NRSV). Some Christians will seek an answer based on clever biblical and theological interpretations, but we can do better, and we owe a modern, sophisticated world a modern, sophisticated answer.

Though many people assume "creation *from nothing*," when the text is read more closely, the biblical support for this understanding is open to some questions. The first Genesis account pictures God not creating from nothing but using existing material to call forth life. "In the beginning when God created the heavens and the earth, the earth was a formless void" (Genesis 1:1–2, NRSV). Read quite literally, the earth was a formless void— already in existence when God began the divine work of calling forth life. The point of the narrative seems to emphasize that God's work is purposeful fertility, the kind of creativity that yields a creation worth calling "good." That purpose would still be valid, the work of God just as necessary for meaningful life, if God began with the existing stuff rather than breathing matter into existence from nothing.

Furthermore, the Hebrew text for "in the beginning" is ambiguous. As it is usually understood, this was *the* beginning, the very beginning, but such a definitive reading is absent from the Hebrew language. The text presents a single word, *bereshith*, which literally just means "beginning." Modifiers must be supplied to this noun, and various translations are possible: "*when* God began to create" or "in *a* beginning" or "*while* beginning." Traditional theology assumes this was the absolute beginning of all time and space and matter, the very beginning, but this interpretation is just that, an *interpretation* of a text that is ambiguous regarding such definitive, scientific details.

Let me invite you to imagine two different concepts of the Creator— the creating, creative God. In one, God literally creates everything that is from the nothing that was. This God speaks, and a rather magical event transpires. Out of thin air, stuff just appears.[22] The material building blocks

22. We might note that such air, taken from a time when there was literally nothing,

of the universe are summoned: carbon, hydrogen, helium, just "poof" into existence. The other conceptualization is a Creator, very different but just as creative, who uses the existing stuff of the material world to call forth true life. In doing so, this God works to endow existence with meaning and purpose.

Even if God did create from nothing, does this necessarily imply that God is an all-powerful creator? The biblical creator might better be described as absolute *creativity* or absolute *newness* or absolute *transformation*. Speaking just in terms of the use of language and logic, a source of creative energy that called life to spring out of nothingness would not necessarily possess (would not theoretically have to possess) all control of that life.

My wife, Amy, and I produced two fully functional human beings. Before there was our relationship, before there was our love, there was nothing. (Our two sons were literally nothing.) The creative union of reproduction brought about two human lives—yet that hardly gives us control over their every thought, action, and decision. A God who creates out of nothing *could* be deemed as having complete control over all things, but that is not a logically or theoretically necessary conclusion. In and of itself the creation narrative does not require creation *ex nihilo*, and, even if we assume creation from nothing, that does not necessarily infer an omnipotent creator. Those are just the most common assumptions derived from interpretation.

On the other hand, assuming that God summons life from existing matter suggests that the divine purpose is less biological and more theological, less physical and more spiritual, less interested in commanding and more prone to loving. In this view, the work of God is less controlling and more luring, less omnipotent and more mysterious presence. A careful, nuanced biblical exegesis might suggest the latter reading is preferable—and even a cursory knowledge of the current scientific worldview might make this understanding a necessity.

In Robert Wright's fascinating book, *Nonzero*, a chapter entitled "You Call This a God?" examines the possibility of God in the universe. Wright's book is essentially on the topic of evolution and is written from a purely secular, if not skeptical/agnostic, perspective. This chapter, however, is full of intrigue and optimism, and he states,

---

would be thinner than our air, which is hardly empty. Stick your hand out of a moving car, and you will feel this truth.

Maybe it is up to us, having inherited only the most ambiguous evidence of divinity, to *construct* clearer evidence in the future. Maybe history is, as various thinkers have suggested, not so much the product of divinity as the realization of divinity—assuming our species is up to the challenge, that is. (One theologian has paraphrased Teilhard [de Chardin] as believing that "God must become for us less Alpha than Omega.")[23]

Pierre Teilhard de Chardin (1881–1955) was a French Jesuit Priest, whose education and work as a paleontologist brought him into some conflict with the Catholic Church. During his lifetime, he was prohibited from publishing his theological ideas, though in recent years Pope Benedict and Pope Francis have spoken favorably of the body of work Teilhard left, much of which was published posthumously. For Teilhard, God was understood as less our beginning point, the source of all the material stuff of our world, and more as the destination to which we are being called. The Divine was seen as the source of the spiritual depth which calls us beyond any biological imperative of our evolutionary development and into the divine *imago Dei* (image of God), by which, alone, we can become fully human.

The God above "God"

All-powerful means a specific thing to modern Christians. It means God's ability to do whatever God pleases, whenever God pleases, however God pleases, whyever God pleases. God is absolute, so no questions can be asked, even when the action or the nonaction of God seems to be unloving, negligent, or even downright wicked. Who are we to question? God is God, and God can do anything. It is this notion of Almighty God that I am arguing against.

I believe we are at a watershed moment in the history of the church. Culture is changing and changing the church with it. What the church, and God, will be is yet to be seen. The affirmations of contemporary science are scarcely known to the average church member. To the degree that scientific affirmations *are* known, many are ignored or ridiculed by large portions of Christianity. The theory of evolution, for example, is lampooned as "just a theory" by many Christians as a way of discounting any evidentiary basis for evolution, even though this is not at all what "theory" means to scientists. A theory is not a fanciful, untested proposition, which may not stand

23. Wright, *Nonzero*, 332.

up to scrutiny. A scientific theory is an accepted hypothesis, an explanation for a particular natural process that has been empirically verified to the extent it can be tested. In other words, science is honest enough to admit that a theory will only hold until it can be proven otherwise. Gravity is just a theory, too. One day it may fail, but, so far, so good!

Some of the findings of science are denounced as deceptions of Satan—who is often regarded as the other power in the universe. Some people of faith even see God's hand at work for the purpose of blinding the unfaithful. Some Christians believe the fossil record is part of God's literal creation, formed at the time of Noah's flood six thousand years ago, for the purpose of appearing millions of years old in order to create the illusion of an evolutionary process. God did this so that only those who read God's word properly, and believe it literally, will know the truth. (You know, you've got to watch that God . . . what a trickster!)

The omnipotence of God has been a cornerstone of traditional theology, but that theology was framed in a prescientific world. For prescientific people God's power-as-force was obvious, unquestioned. A plentiful harvest was the blessing of the all-powerful God. The famine was God's curse. Storm and plague, every blessing and every tragedy was the direct initiative of a God who could do everything. But scientific knowledge has changed this, for everyone, forever. Most people no longer consider a lightning bolt or natural calamity as an expression of God's anger. Most modern people have given up these superstitions, even though many have not given up the idea that the *good* fortunes of life sometimes come as the direct intervention of God. Too many people are quick to affirm God's hand in their blessings without recognizing that if this is so, it must also be true that every tragedy is sent from God.

In his commentary on the text of Luke 13, William Loader says, "Even very traditional, respectable and respectful citizens come to the point where they have to recognize bastardry for what it is and stop attributing everything to God."[24] A scientific worldview should make it more difficult to assign to God's specific handiwork the day-to-day affairs of our lives, because we understand cosmology and meteorology and biology, the immutable laws of nature and the random mutation which is at the heart of evolutionary process.

Christians have now affirmed the Copernican world, with our sun as the center of one of many solar systems, and a Newtonian world with its

24. Loader, "First Thoughts on Year C," para. 4.

fundamental natural laws—which have yielded the scientific method. Science discovered these worlds in separate eras, even though each came with its charges of heresy, and each shattered God in the process. With each new discovery, every new paradigm of understanding, the "God above God"[25] survived. A similar realignment is happening again, and even though it takes a great deal of time, humans will again adjust our vision.

Until the modern period it was not completely possible to rule out God from the process of creation. Some things were not understood, could not be explained, so God remained a workable hypothesis, even to those in the scientific community who were skeptical. But the advances of modern physics have even changed that. The mathematics of cosmology can now justify a creation without a creator, the motion of evolution without a first mover, the fact of a very big bang without a cause. I do not understand this. I cannot begin to explain it. What I do know is that this conjecture is not just a theory, and the scientific establishment is not going to retreat from this any more than it will announce next week that the common cold is actually a divine plague instead of the manifestation of the rhinovirus.

It will take time for the evidence of the "godless creation," which is the basic story of evolution, to filter through the halls of academia and finally be understood enough to be accepted at the grass roots level. Truth travels slowly. Though many still do not accept it, evolution has been an undisputed scientific fact, and the basis of all subsequent biological study, for nearly two hundred years. This should not be surprising, as human trafficking (slavery) is still being practiced throughout the world.

As our family experienced several years ago, guides in a cave in West Virginia still point out the fossils and explain that they were embedded in the cave's roof six thousand years ago, "at the time of Noah's flood." Yes, truth travels slowly. So, it will take the church some time to adjust its understanding of God, but this must be done. As has been the case numerous times in the church's past, as it adapts to a new understanding, God will be with us along the way.

God has not died, and God will not, not at the hand of science nor any other human discipline of study and discovery, but the understanding that "God" refers to a Supreme Being, external to the physical world, who literally spoke atoms into existence, who still controls hurricanes and

---

25. Paul Tillich says, "The ultimate source of the courage to be is the 'God above God'; this is the result of our demand to transcend theism." *Courage to Be*, 186.

tornadoes, who can heal your dying grandmother, if God chooses, etc., that understanding will die—just not soon enough.

The God who is *not* all-powerful does not cease to be God, nor cease to transform human beings in the most significant ways. A new understanding of the Divine, however, has at least the potential to make God rational, believable in our scientific world. Of equal importance, the vision of this "new God" should put an end to the perpetuation of violence, at least to any violence which can be justified in the name of God.

Above our most carefully conceived doctrines of God, our best attempts to understand the Mystery, our fledgling efforts to share that experience, above our limited words and our limited thoughts, above it all is the God who is above. True God is above the God we think we know. God always will be. Atheism is often the rejection of a God poorly understood, of good theology greatly misunderstood. Science cannot disprove or destroy the God who is above God. It is the true God—who is more faith than fact, more preposition than proposition,[26] more myth than math, more Spirit than science—the God who can only be experienced, not explained, to whom humanity must give our commitments and our devotion.

"God is above all and through all and in all" (Eph 4:4–6 NRSV).

GOD. Always. Does. Everything. God. Can. Do.

---

26. I will explain this reference in the concluding chapter.

3

God. **ALWAYS**. Does. Everything. God. Can. Do. (God beneath Us)

"God is the energy in all things, always working for the good." (Rom 8:28)[1]

The cure for pulpit dullness is not brilliance, but reality—albeit a much bigger reality than we imagined, bigger than history or psychology, so big that it transfigures everything we so confidently named "reality."

RICHARD LISCHER[2]

1. This is my own translation, which I will use throughout the rest of the book.
2. Lischer, *End of Words*, 126.

Questions to Prompt Your Reading

How much of your potential have you realized? If you have not reached full potential, why not?

What would it mean to be able to live a fully actualized life?

When you think of the word eternity, which word in each pair of words best corresponds with your understanding?

Length or Depth
Infinite or Ultimate
Quantity or Quality
Mathematics or Mystery

What is the most sensational experience you've ever had? Have you ever tried to tell about it or write about it? Can words convey your experience?

Do you believe in the omni*presence* of God? Have you ever felt at a distance from God, or sensed the absence of God? How do you reconcile any conflict between your two answers?

Does God answer prayers? Does that mean that the person praying gets what they want?

Potential

In 1996 we moved to Birmingham, Alabama. After paying $84,000 for our first home, a cozy one story, wooden bungalow in Clemson, South Carolina, the first house we priced in the Magic City was, wait for it . . . $335,000. Housing has increased even more precipitously since we became homeowners, but at the time this was a truly shocking number. Apparently, we were not in Kansas anymore! So, it took a lot of looking, but we did finally find a place. The realtor said it was perfect. Because it was the lowest priced home in the neighborhood, with a little bit of work it would benefit from that first rule of real estate: location, location, location. Especially since I've been known to use a hammer, to take out a few walls, our realtor felt the little "fixer-upper" was just right. "It has . . . potential," he said. Well, three years later, and a lot of cleaning, gallons of paint, another wall removed, a new bathroom added, and a *lot* of sweat, when we finally sat down to relax, Amy said, "I don't ever want to buy a house with *potential* again!" Amen, sister. Give me a home that is fully actualized, a home with all its potential realized. (To be sure, this has not stopped my wife from dreaming up renovation ideas for every single home we've lived in since, but it is a nice theory.)

Like fixer-up houses, human beings are filled with potential, often unfulfilled potential. Another conviction of faith, however, an idea as universal as the omnipotence of God, is the understanding of the perfection of God, the completeness of God. So, while humans have plenty of room for improvement, there is no such unrealized possibility in God. God *is*. There is nothing yet to be fulfilled, nothing lacking. There is no potential in God, only actualized *Godness*.

What more could God be? What more could God do?

There has never been a moment since God said, "Let there be . . ." that God has not been God, doing everything God can do, being everything God can be. When did God start being God? The traditional belief is that before time was, God already is. When will God stop being God? The traditional theological affirmation is that after the consummation of all things, when there will be no earth, no time, nothing at all, God still will be. God always has been and always will be.

God is.

Always. Infinity. Eternity. Quantity and Quality.

"Always" is a difficult word to truly comprehend because we have so little experience with it. The old adage has it right: "The only thing that stays the same is that everything changes." Nothing is forever. There is no "always" in our world. (Well, death and taxes, but nothing else!) Clothes go out of style, unless you keep them long enough for them to become fashionable again. "BFF," taken from the lexicon of social media, means "best friends forever," but they seldom are. Music changes. The Beatles, who? In a world where technology moves at the speed of light, don't even try to keep up. And, speaking of the speed of light, two papers were published in March 2013 in the *European Physics Journal D* that indicate even this measurement, which for a long time has been understood to be an unwavering constant throughout the entire universe, may not be so constant, after all.[3] Einstein long ago proved that time, itself, is relative. So . . . always?

"Always" brings to mind the concept of infinity, which brings to mind the philosophers' old saw about the monkey at the typewriter. Leave him there for long enough, and eventually, just by happenstance, one monkey would correctly type every book ever produced in human literature. Every word, every space, every comma, every period, randomly typed, but every character, finally in its correct place. Can you even imagine? But that's infinity.

In theological terms, John Newton tried to convey infinity as he envisioned eternal life with God. His "Amazing Grace" is immortalized among Christians, and the final verse attempts to define "always." "When we've been there ten thousand years, bright shining as the sun, we've no less days to sing God's praise, than when we first begun!"[4] Infinity is one of those concepts that hurts your head if you think about it long enough, but God, we say, always has been and always will be.

God is.

Linear time, however, may not be the best way to think of God. Infinity or eternity may not only refer to a quantity. Maybe there is a better way to measure the infinite. In his sermons and lectures at Mountain Brook Baptist Church in Birmingham, the late Dr. William E. Hull taught that eternity is not a quantity, but a quality. Maybe eternal life with God is not supposed to denote a linear measure of infinite time ("When we've been

---

3. Emspak, "Speed of Light," para. 4.

4. Newton, John. "Amazing Grace!"

there ten thousand years . . ."), but a depth of life, a fullness of experience, the ripeness of time. The Greeks referred to linear time by the word *chronos*, but to the fullness of time by the word *kairos*, even though both words are translated by the English word "time." If we can wrap our heads around this distinction, we may begin to conceive of God not as a Being, acting here and there, now and then, this time, that time, and the next time, but as a movement or Spirit, filling all that is with the depth of divine fullness.[5]

In his extended poem *The Prophet*, the Khalil Gibran speaks of death this way: "What is it to die but to free the breath of its restless tides, to rise and expand and seek God forever."[6] This image doesn't depend on quantity, singing God's praise for ten thousand years, and that only as a beginning. The image challenges us to consider a different kind of eternity. Death may generally be conceived as the end of breathing, blowing out one last quantitative breath, one final exhale. Gibran says, with contradictory vision, eternity is an infinite inhale, which is no quantity at all. Imagine what we might experience if we could inhale forever! With this picture we are introduced to a way to think about eternity without drawing upon mathematics at all. "Eternity" and "always" become theological computations, not mathematical ones.

The "always" of "God always does everything God can do" should not be thought of in mathematical terms, as if what is important is tallying God's work, finally adding together a string of infinitely long divine miracles, thereby proving God's faithfulness. "Always" means that because God never started being God, God could never cease that divine vocation, and because God *is*, there can never be an experience that is not already bathed in grace and goodness and love. Even in horrific happenings, natural or human evil, God is with us. Always.

The Power and Problem of Words (Again)

As stated in the last chapter, it is the human attempt to express the experience of God in limited, human language, to communicate an understanding, even to define "God," that has created so many of the world's problems

---

5. I served as a colleague of Bill Hull for four years, where he became one of the most important mentors I have ever had. My reflection on Bill's understanding of eternity is a composite, composed from my memory of his sermons and studies, and several private conversations.

6 Gibran, *Prophet*, 81.

regarding religion. Religious beliefs, doctrines, and dogmas spring from the felt need to put the intangible experiences of God into concrete words. If these words can point to the originating experience, they serve an invaluable purpose, but too often the words get substituted for the experience, as if the words or the doctrines and dogmas are themselves holy.

In her book *Encountering God,* Diana Eck writes,

> Our concept of God is not simply given; we learn it, for better or worse. We develop the operative concept with which we live, inheriting God, as it were, from our historical religious tradition as it is taught to us. Learning something of God from our families and teachers, from personal friends and public figures, we develop an impression of what this word "God" means.[7]

As I began writing this book, I took a week of study leave to ride and write. I took my Harley Davidson 1200 Sportster to the mountains and spent mornings and evenings writing, but I spent the middle hours of each day in the wind. I rode some of the best motorcycle and sports car roads in North Carolina, most of which now bear some silly nickname in order to promote the economy all along these serpentine paths. Crisscrossing the Blue Ridge Parkway, I put five hundred miles on "The Snake," "The Devil's Whip," "The Diamondback," and "The Rattler."

As I rode, I was thinking about God, and words about God, about riding, and words about riding, and I contemplated how I might tell someone who had never been on a motorcycle, much less on a Harley on NC Highway 80, what that all out sensory experience is like. There is nothing about that thrill that can be conveyed linguistically. Even the smells of North Carolina's mountains defy literary description. How would you help someone experience with words alone the sweetness of honeysuckle and the freshness of sassafras, the bitter aroma of boxwoods that dot some of the mountainsides, or the spruce and fir Christmas trees that cover others?

Riding the open ridges, the dense forests, the flowered meadows, and the expansive valleys, the difference is dramatic, almost intoxicating, but is this an experience I could ever truly convey to someone without a functioning olfactory gland? Could I even explain this to an experienced biker, but one who had never been on those particular roads at that particular time of the year? I love to read exceptional, descriptive writing—but even the very best of writers cannot fully condense such a sensory experience into words on paper. And, much beyond the exhilarating experience of riding a Harley

7. Eck, *Encountering God,* 48.

in the Blue Ridge Mountains, the spiritual experience of the Divine has an ineffable character. By definition that experience is, well . . . it's ineffable!

Because the experience of God is so moving, in so many cases life-changing, it is understandable that humans have always sought to put this experience into words. This is as it should be. The problem comes when we begin to worship the words, to grant them an inerrant character they were never intended, an aspiration they could never attain. The church has identified grandiose terms to speak of a grandiose experience, of a grandiose God, but these terms and their related concepts often overwhelm us, confuse our thinking. For example, many of us who were raised in the church were taught of God's "omni-attributes": God is omnipotent (all-powerful), omnipresent (all present), and omniscient (all knowing).

Most of the people I know say they believe in God. That belief should provide comfort and strength. Jesus's example was in knowing God in the tender relationship of an Abba, the Aramaic term for papa or daddy, yet this experience is not true for many believers. Despite what they *say*, many people live with the unease of a God who is always watching, threatening, judging, and who feels unreachably distant especially in times of great need.

The prophets and the psalmists expressed this experience of existential loneliness as they often raised a figurative fist and cried, "Where are you, God? How long, O Lord? Why?" These are the words of people whose own lived experience does not, at times, match what they say they believe.

If anyone truly believed in the omnipresence of God, how could they ever cry, "Where is God?" How is it possible to reconcile the belief in God's omnipresence with Jesus's experience, that agony when he cried in pain and alienation, "My God, My God, why have you forsaken me?" (Matt 27:46 NRSV)? God is omnipresent, yet even Jesus experienced the forsakenness, the total absence of God. These are some of the most difficult words in the Bible, and Christian commentators have wrestled with this "cry of dereliction" for centuries. Where was God? Had God truly absconded?

"Where is God?" is a cry of the soul. It is the reflexive, predictable response of deep pain. There is no shame in uttering such a primal scream in the face of life's bitter disappointments, so it is important to formulate our theology in moments of strength and clarity. In doing so, when tragedy comes, and it will, we can recognize that cry for what it is. It is essential to have a faith built on affirmations that will sustain us, even in "the valley of the shadow of death" (Ps 23:4 NRSV).

"Always" means never having to ask, "Where is God?" Yes, that experience is real enough, even Jesus knew it, but people of faith should arm themselves with the confidence that God is never apart from us, so when challenge and suffering and death come, this will be a truth to which we may cling. It may be all we have. The apostle Paul makes this clear in his soaring affirmation: "*Nothing* can separate us from the love of God" (Rom 8:38–39 NRSV; emphasis added).

Nothing Can Separate Us and the Irony of Intervention

Paul's affirmation notwithstanding, there is something many people of faith do not seem to understand about the word "nothing." No time. No place. No circumstance. Nothing can separate us. God is always with us. Standing in Athens, speaking to the highly religious pagans of that city, Paul quotes one of their own philosophers: "In [God] we live and move and have our being" (Acts 17:28 NRSV).

Paul's theology affirms that we are bathed in God. (We Baptists might prefer to say *immersed* in God!) I believe the reality of God is the heart of all that is. I believe God *is*. I believe God is always all-God, yet it is shocking to some people when I tell them I do not believe in an interventionist God. They look at me as if I am some kind of heretic, as if I don't believe in God at all. On the contrary, I think of my position as a *more*-God position, and a more biblical one, even than the belief of my critics. If we live in God, move in God, have our being in God, if "nothing can separate us from the love of God" (Rom 3:31 NRSV), why would God ever need to intervene? How *could* God ever intervene? Intervene? From where? To where?

In his manuscript for an Advent sermon entitled "God in a Song," Dr. John Ballenger writes these words:

> So, you see, there is in this season of Advent,
> a certain inappropriateness
> to singing "Come, Oh Come Immanuel."
> For if Immanuel is Immanuel—God with us,
> then God doesn't—God can't come, for God is here.
> And if we sing "Come, Oh Come," it's not God-with-us we really affirm.
> It's like the invocation, right?
> We're not invoking God's presence. God is here.
> We're invoking our own selves to what's real—to who's here.
> So, when we sing, "Come, Oh Come," it's our own selves
> we want to come to the God who is here.

42

Unless, of course, we add nuance to the song I'm not sure is there,
and think within the truth of God with us,
we're always being called into the bigger picture—
the bigger grace—the bigger love.
We get enough to know we want more,
and that there's both more to want
and more to know.
Come God who is with us come even more.[8]

In my experience, despite what they say, most people do not really believe God is omnipresent. Their prayers reveal this. It has been said that if you want to know what someone truly believes, you should listen to them pray. What most people pray in times of need sounds a lot like, "I know you are far away, God, but I need you to get down here and do something. Now!"

Divine intervention is the heart and soul of belief for many people. It is the reason for prayer: God exists as a Supernatural Being, out there, up there in heaven, and intervenes when we pray—if we pray correctly, if we are faithful, if we are righteous enough, and, if God chooses to. And if God does not intervene, well, God just doesn't, and since God is God, and we're not, we do not have any right to ask why not, and we're certainly not smart enough to understand. Isn't this how people speak of the divine intervention in which they so earnestly believe?

It's hard to imagine a worse, more destructive theology. There are several possible outcomes to such belief, and the prayers that emerge from such belief. All are unfortunate. First, if God does not intervene, many people choose to believe they are at fault, that they are not faithful enough or good enough or that God does not love them enough, because of something they have done. They believe this because low self-esteem may just be the original sin. Or they believe this because in various ways other people, pastors, teachers, or friends tell them they are not good enough. This theology is just as bad, just as wrong, and just as harmful as it was a couple thousand years ago when Job's friends confronted him using the conventional wisdom of their day—which has not changed—to blame him for his troubles.

Eliphaz said Job was being punished. Whether Job could admit it or not, obviously he was in the wrong: "Who that was innocent ever perished?" (Job 4:7 NRSV). Bildad claimed Job was being tested by God: "If you are pure and upright, surely God will rouse up for you" (Job 8:6

8. Ballenger, "God in a Song."

NRSV). Zophar, rounding out the triumvirate of such friendly comfort, said his friend was suffering because it was God's will, and we should never question God's will: "Can you find out the deep things of God?" (Job 11:7 NRSV). Those three responses of the friends are still as common as the falling rain: it's your fault . . . you are being tested . . . everything happens for a reason, that you're just not smart enough to understand.

As it has for thousands of years, an interventionist theology inflicts pain on people, usually at a time when such a belief only compounds their need.

Another inevitable, consequential response when God does not intervene is for people to blame God. A God who could, but just does not protect the innocent or heal the weak or save the dying is a God many people cannot love and will not tolerate—and for good reason.

I was walking the hallway of the hospital one day when I encountered a young woman. We engaged in conversation, and her story broke my heart, mostly because it has been repeated countless times. She and her husband were actively involved in a large evangelical church and attending a young couples' class at the time all the other couples seemed to be getting pregnant. "The Lord has blessed us," someone would say every week in Sunday school, which is another way of saying "God intervened." In those words of celebration, she could only hear "and God is *not* blessing me." Over time that lack of blessing became harder to bear, until she slowly began to hear, "God blessed them, and God is cursing us. Why?"

That church could not provide answers that did not continue to inflict blame on this young couple, and it had no other concept of God to provide. She hasn't been in church since. She may not have given up her actual belief in God, but, practically speaking, this is exactly what has happened. Who needs a God who chooses capriciously or punitively whom to bless and whom to curse? She did not.

Of course, sometimes people pray and get just what they want. Ironically, this may be an unfortunate outcome. In the big picture, the unintended consequence of "God answered my prayer!" is that this praise fosters the celebration of the God who has supposedly intervened. That belief, in turn, inflicts more people, like the young woman in the hospital, for whom God has not intervened. This celebration further fosters the notion of the distant-but-all-powerful God who chooses whom to bless and whom to curse. In the process, the people whose prayers are not answered often learn to hate themselves. Either way, it's God who gets a black eye.

The word intervene comes from two Latin roots. *Venire* means "to come," and *inter* is a prefix meaning "between." To intervene is "to come between," but what could possibly come between us and a God in whom "we live and move and have our being" (Acts 17:28 NRSV). Ironically, an interventionist theology may do less to affirm the presence of God than to create a distance between us. Nothing can separate us—except a theology that convinces us otherwise.

"Always" means there is never a time God is separated from us. When we get what we want, and when we do not; when we get what we need, and when we will not; when God "answers" our prayers, and when we pray to the silence . . . we are not separated.

God is with us. Always.

Beneath the movement of life there is a deep river of mystery and meaning. Like the frequencies played on a bass subwoofer, it is a frequency that is felt and not heard. The affirmation of faith over the centuries still resonates to those who are attentive to this movement, and not just looking for sensational miracles: "The eternal God is thy refuge, and underneath are the everlasting arms" (Deut 33:27).

"Nothing can separate us."

The Energy in All Things

Romans 8:28 is one of those verses of Scripture that shows up often in the theology of the prosperity gospel, which I have identified in this chapter without specifically naming it. The prosperity gospel, which can be identified as far back as the Deuteronomic theology of the Old Testament, teaches that God blesses with health, wealth, and prosperity those who are faithful. Or, as it can be read in Rom 8:28: "And we know that in all things *God works* for the good of those *who love him*" (NIV; emphases added). In other words, *if* you love God, God will intervene and bless you.

Maybe we have misunderstood.

It is easy to read into this text the transactional relationship the prosperity gospel proclaims: *if* you love God, *then* God will bless you. It's an old, old idea. I am afraid it came to us from a much more superstitious age, an age of warring and jealous tribal gods, an age of fear in which the gods were to be appeased by any means: offerings, tributes, sacrifices, even human sacrifices.

Is God so petty? Is our relationship so transactional? Is faith really a matter of "do this . . . get that"? Does God only respond if we make an offering, something so valuable that even the Divine can be moved? If you love God with valuable offerings, *then* God intervenes? Do we relate to parents or loved ones, respected friends, with such tit for tat insecurity? Do we offer help to our children only if they ask and ask correctly? Do we support them only if they "prepay" with some valuable commodity? Do we save our children from harm only if they ask first, and then only if they ask with appropriate deference?

We need to hear this prosperity theology stated so dramatically that we can hear how primitive and unfortunate such an understanding is. As ancient Israel was breaking free of their tribal, polytheistic past, the prophets offered a new understanding. Speaking to a faithful but fearful people, eight centuries before Christ, the prophet Micah asked and answered the questions I've just asked. He spoke dramatically. We need to hear it again today:

> "With what shall I come before the Lord, and bow myself before God on high? Shall I come before [God] with burnt offerings, with calves a year old? Will the Lord be pleased with thousands of rams, with ten thousands of rivers of oil? Shall I give my firstborn for my transgression, the fruit of my body for the sin of my soul?"
>
> [No!]
>
> [God] has told you, O mortal, what is good, and what does the Lord require of you but to do justice and to love kindness and to walk humbly with your God? (Mic 6:6–9 NRSV)

Micah is clear. God needs no transaction. No gift, not even a firstborn child is enough to buy God's affection—because that is not how God works. God loves. We just need to live, justly, kindly, humbly. There is no tit for tat in love—yet, as so many people hear Rom 8, if "*God works* for the good of those *who love him*," I am afraid it is easy to hear exactly the kind of theology the prosperity preachers have always proclaimed. As with all Scripture, however, there is more than one way to read—a more helpful way to interpret.

In the phrase "God works for the good," the Greek word translated "works" is the verb *sunergein*. *Sun* is the preposition "with," and you can hear in the noun *energein* its English cognates, "ergonomic" and "energy." Thinking of God as a force of work or an "energy with" may help us better understand Paul's affirmation to the Romans. I believe the NRSV is more helpful, with "all things *work together* for good," and Eugene Peterson's translation is better still: "Every detail in our lives of love for God *is worked into something good.*"

My own translation is "God is the *energy in* all things [*sunergein*], *always working* for the good." God is not some Divine Bystander, a Supernatural Being watching from a distance, waiting to be sought with fear, demanding to be appeased appropriately. God is the Spirit of good, the energy of love, working among us, never apart from us.

Addressing the illuminating theology of Teilhard de Chardin, whose theology was framed by his understandings as an evolutionary scientist, Ilia Delio describes the Teilhardian concept of "Omega" this way:

> Omega is like the quantum potential in that it subsists throughout nature as . . . the principle of integrated wholeness. It is present from the beginning of the Big Bang and is the goal of evolution. . . . Teilhard identified this deep personal presence of concentrating energy—Omega—with the ultimate depth of love we name God. Thus he breaks open a new understanding of God and matter through the energy of love.[9]

While religion is not obliged to answer to science, neither should it be in constant conflict. To be sure, standing in opposition to the scientific academy, and in diametric contradiction to the laws of nature, has not served the church well over the centuries. The notion of a Being, removed from time and space until deciding to intervene, acting by divine fiat in ways that can contradict the laws of nature, this kind of God cannot be reconciled with a current scientific understanding. The church must, once again, come to grips with this disconnect, and be aware of the danger that holding such a view proves to the people and the institution.

The strange language of quantum science, however, says that the stuff of the entire universe is connected in deep ways, perhaps through the buzzing of underlying strings of energy. Even though God the Intervener can no longer be harmonized with our understandings of the physical world, I believe God the Energy in All Things might be. This God—who is still God!—is a real presence, a true source of influence, a momentum for good, the mysterious Spirit, always with us, always working, always seeking the good . . . I believe that kind of God can, *and does*, exist in our strange world, not intervening, but working even more pervasively, always working for the good.

9. Delio, *Unbearable Wholeness of Being*, 41.

"God is the energy in all things, always working for the good" (Rom 8:28).

God. **ALWAYS.** Does. Everything. God. Can. Do.

AN ASIDE: PRAYER

"Pray for my soul. More things are wrought by prayer | Than this world dreams of: Wherefore, let thy voice | Rise like a fountain for me night and day."[1]

Those famous words are spoken by King Arthur, in Tennyson's epic poem, "Idylls of the King." Dying words of a legendary king speak the sure conviction of many: "Things are wrought by prayer . . ." To quote the KJV, "the effectual fervent prayer of a righteous man availeth much" (Jas 5:16), or, in a more common vernacular, "prayer changes things."

To be a "true believer" means knowing that if you believe enough, "whatever you ask . . . you will receive" (Matt 21:22 NRSV). Whatever you ask—which means, anything, anything at all: strength for the time of trial, a new job, the healing of mama's cancer, even that new, shiny Cadillac! "Believe!" the preachers say. "Pray!" It will be given to you.

This is what prayer means for many. Even if most haven't gotten the Cadillac of their prayer, the literal reading of a few Scriptures, and a belief in the unquestioned omnipotence of God, have led many people of faith to this understanding of prayer.

God is the source of all power, and prayer is the means of manipulating that power, for our own good, so answered prayer is the proof, like a mathematical formula: Believe + Ask = Get!

I once shared this power of the God who can't with a family member. Genuinely puzzled, he asked, "So, if you think God can't do what you want, why would you ever pray?"

Do you hear it? Do you hear what I heard, that common understanding of the focus of prayer, the intrinsically self-centered nature of praying?

If God can't do what *I want* . . . why would I ever pray at all?

---

1. Tennyson, "Idylls of the King," line 415.

I tried to answer carefully. I have no need to scold or shame. I also know prayer so often comes from experiences of deep hurt: we cry out to God out of the deepest anguish. That is as it should be, but if our fundamental understanding is that prayer is simply the "exploitation of the divine," I fear we have missed something essential.[2]

That quotation is from Thomas Moore, who explains his understanding this way:

> A billboard near an old house of mine displayed in six-foot type: PRAY. IT WORKS. I always thought this was the ultimate in American pragmatism. If it doesn't work, do you stop praying? What does it mean to say that prayer works? You get what you want? Life gets better?
>
> My billboard would say: PRAY. IT MAY NOT WORK. Prayer is an alternative to working hard to get what you want. One discovers eventually that what you want is almost always what you don't need.
>
> Pray—period! Don't expect anything. Or better, expect nothing. Prayer cleanses us of expectations and allows holy will, providence, and life itself an entry. What could be more worth the effort—or the noneffort?[3]

Let that sink in. Prayer is not pragmatic asking, it is communication. It is communion with the presence, not manipulation of the power. If we could learn to pray that way, it would change . . . everything.

2. Moore, *Meditations*, 69.
3. Moore, *Meditations*, 69.

4

God. Always. **Does.** Everything. God. Can. Do. (God around Us)

"I am that I am." (Exod 3:14 NRSV)

Nothing in nature looks like cloud by day and fire by night except a volcano. The depth of the Lord God's compelling but contradictory power is well evoked by the extraordinary image of a volcano brought into a tent.

Jack Miles[1]

1. Miles, *God: A Biography*, 126.

51

Questions to Prompt Your Reading

Where have you seen God at work? How do you know it was God?

Moses asked God's name, and God said, "I am." What do you make of this name?

Thinking of naming God, what name(s) do you use? (Lord, Father, Mother, Spirit . . .) How much does the name shape your understanding of who God is and what God does?

What is the difference in doing and being? In your own life? For the life and work and presence of God?

What do you expect God to do? In crises? In everyday moments? In your life? In history?

Does God intervene in human history? Define intervene.

Can you think of a time someone was present for you in a moment of real need? What did they do? How did their presence change your situation?

The Meaning of "Is" and "I Am"

In what is now a rather infamous episode from the presidential administration of Bill Clinton, the president was responding to a withering series of indicting questions from the grand jury. He was being tried for impeachment, resulting from an illicit extramarital affair conducted while in office. Clinton testified that he was not lying when he had said, referring to the woman with whom he had the affair, "There's nothing going on between us." He was rebuffed by the jury: How could that have been a true statement? His famous reply may outlive the forty-second president of the United States: "It depends on what the meaning of the word 'is' is."[2]

What is "is"?

God is.

When Moses was humbled by that mysterious burning bush in the desert, took off his shoes and bowed there, he finally mustered a simple question, stuttering through fear and awe: "Wh-wh-what is y-y-y-your n-name?" The divine answer has reverberated through time, and, as many names do, reveals deep insight into the character and nature of Moses's God, who became the God of Jesus. Known as the tetragrammaton (literally, "four letters"), the divine name is transliterated, YHVH. In ancient Hebrew no vowels are supplied in the text, and the Jews came to revere this name so greatly that rabbinic teaching prohibited that it be spoken at all. Instead, the vowels from the word *Adonai*, another Hebrew name for God (literally, "Lord"), were applied to the consonants of the divine name, resulting in the name, YaHVeH—Yahweh—which is how Jews have spoken of this one "who must not be named,"[3] YHVH, ever since. From this name Christians also derived the name, a kind of crude substitute, Jehovah.

The fascinating and revealing aspect of the name is that it shares the root of the Hebrew verb "to be" (*lihiyot*). In that ancient narrative God answers Moses, providing the name by telling Moses, "Tell the Pharaoh that 'I Am' has sent you" (Exod 3:14 NRSV). This reference has been a source of confusion for centuries, but there may be no more important clue into the nature of the Divine than this. As the son of two English majors, and a particularly grammar-conscious father, I learned early to conjugate, and I learned all the parts of speech of the verb "to be": am, is, are, was, were, be,

2. Noah, "Bill Clinton," para. 2.

3. In the *Harry Potter* series, Harry's perennial nemesis, Lord Voldemort, was referred to throughout the novels, due to his notorious wickedness as "He-Who-Must-Not-Be-Named."

being, been. It may not be incorrect, then, to suggest that what God said to Moses was, "Tell the Pharaoh that I Am-Is-Are-Was-Were-Be-Being-Been has sent you," or, in a much abbreviated form, "Tell the Pharaoh that 'Is' has sent you."

I played middle school football in a small South Carolina town and had a reasonably successful one season career as a starting quarterback, before giving up directing the offense for playing my trumpet. Those days are far away, and were few even as they lasted, but the memories are still potent. I can still taste that plastic mouthpiece which on hot days seemed more a choking liability than a dental asset. I can still smell one hundred yards of well-kept Bermuda, which smells much sweeter when you're tearing through the cheerleaders' banner for a Thursday night game than when you're lying face down in it with six linemen piled on top of you. I still remember the cadence of the snap count and the rhythm of calling plays in the huddle: "thirty-six-power bootleg on two, ready break." And though I've lost touch with nearly all my teammates, their names and faces will die with me.

One particularly good lineman was a favorite of the team. He was affable and hardworking, but apparently his dad wasn't as much a stickler for correct grammar as mine was. I'll never forget the day after practice when a teammate asked who was going to the party the next night after our game, and he shouted, "I'm is!" This grammatical disaster in a smelly locker room may be the perfect translation of God's most important declaration: I am *Is*.

God Is. Or, maybe even better: God. Is.

More, much more has certainly been said of God, but I wonder if there is anything more that *needs* to be said? Is saying more about God not ultimately a detriment, an affront, a polluting of what and who God really is? Speaking in general terms of the praise reflected in the Psalms, and specifically in Ps 23, Stephen Mitchell says,

> The praise is addressed to whom? To what? When gratitude wells up through our whole body, we don't even ask. Words such as God and Tao and Buddha-nature only point to the reality that is the source and essence of all things, the luminous intelligence that shines from the depths of the human heart: the vital, immanent, subtle, radiant X. The ancient Jews named this unnamable reality yhvh, "that which causes [everything] to exist," or, even more insightfully, ehyeh, "I am." Yet God is neither here nor there, neither

before nor after, neither outside nor inside. As soon as we say that God is anything we are a billion light-years away.[4]

If we could have understood the simplicity, and the complexity of "God Is," over the centuries, so much abuse in the name of God could have been prevented. Rather than trying to carefully delineate who and what and where God is and what God does and how God does it and what God would have us to do and when and where and why . . . what if we just said, "God Is"? How many of the schisms within religious institutions are the results of different understandings of the nature and working of God? All of them? How many conflicts involving religious institutions, between religions and other institutions, and between one religion and another, result from conflicting views of God? All of them?

In her book, *A Vocabulary of Faith*, Kathleen Norris addresses the issue:

> I have begun to see the commandments in the light of an underlying covenant, as essential to the relationship that God is establishing with us. . . . Any relationship, to remain alive, requires at least two living participants. In this case, a God who does not exist as a convenience, magically giving us what we want, or feel we deserve, but a God who simply IS—the ground of being, the great "I Am." And with this God, experienced . . . as "the living God" (Jeremiah 10.10, NRSV), we can come into our own, no longer in fear of "being nothing."[5]

God made it rather simple: "I Am." There is divine presence in this world. Period. Speaking to the weary and wearying question of the existence of God, in his book *Days of Awe and Wonder*, Marcus Borg says,

> The question of God's existence is no longer about whether there is another being in addition to the universe. Rather, the question becomes: What is "is-ness"? What is "what is"? What is reality? [Is there] a "more"?[6]

The answer of the people of faith is, yes! There is a *more*. God is the more. God Is.

Is there any deeper confession of faith than that? It is we, human beings, who have created the difficulties by developing complex theologies,

4. Mitchell, *Book of Psalms*, xiv.
5. Norris, *Vocabulary of Faith*, 86–87.
6. Borg, *Days of Awe and Wonder*, 37.

which do originate in an experience of the divine, but the expression of which is always dependent upon a human interpretation of that experience.

God Is.

The definitions of God, the interpretations of those definitions of God, and the beliefs and dogmas and practices of those who believe in the God they have so defined, are humanly conceived. I do believe in revelation, inspiration, the movement of God in and through specific people and events, but anything said to be "of God" must be filtered through human understanding and interpretation, and through human communication. Inspiration is the work of God. Theology, the written form of that inspiration, is a human product.

If we could contemplate the beauty of the simple affirmation of God, "I am" (God Is), rather than rely on complex dogmas, so much of the human anxiety about God and our relationship with God might just vanish. When bad things happen to good people,[7] those who are affected too often cry out, "Why? What is God doing? Why did God let that happen? Where is God?"

Why can we not simply answer, "God Is"?

In despair, and often in response to the misdeeds of religious people, or religions themselves, people turn away from a God whose actions they can no longer see in biblical proportion, whose miraculous touch has evaded them, avoided them. In these moments of spiritual crisis, disbelief overcomes faith, and they give up on the existence of a God who does not act as they think God should act: there is no God. God is not.

Why can we not simply answer, "God Is"?

In moments of crisis, people of faith gather to pray, but the angst behind the prayer is so often unfortunate, unhealthy. "We need God," they say. "Why isn't God doing something, now?"

Why can we not simply answer, "God Is"?

Of course, I would never make this statement to any individual, or to any family in a moment of crisis, which requires pastoral care, not theological instruction, but the questions I can ask here are: What more do we really want God to do? What is God not doing that God could do? God is God. God Is. How is that not enough?

If God is the source of life, if "God is love" (1 John 4:8 NRSV), if God *Is*, what more could God *be*? If the very nature of God is "is-ness," if God is

---

7. The title of Rabbi Harold Kushner's book is, *Why Bad Things Happen to Good People.*

"be-ing" itself, if "God" is a verb (which is by definition, action), how could *Is* ever cease *doing* something?

God Is.

Being and Doing

The issue may be that we simply want more than can be done, especially in times of dire need. This is understandable. In the crises of life, in the crush of bitter pain, we cannot bear to think the unthinkable, so the thought process is understandable: How can this be? This is not fair! Something must change! Do something. *Someone. Do. Something!*

The lesson each of us learns, eventually, is that life is not fair. "All true stories end in death."[8] This may be the hardest lesson of all, but who wants to believe this? Maybe God can do something. Surely *God* can do something, right?

If God is pure Being, however, what else does God need to be *doing*? This may seem a ridiculously philosophical question, one with no ground in practical reality, but dis-ease with a distinction in *being* and *doing* may indicate a shallow understanding or a selfish insecurity. In an American culture steeped in the productivity of our "Protestant work ethic," we are programmed to equate worth with work: your identity and value are equivalent to what you do, specifically, what you produce.

Biblical wisdom values work, but it locates the essential goodness of the human creature not in what we have done, but in what *God* has done. Our blessedness is a virtue, not of what we do, but of who we *are*. God created us in the divine image, and before we had a chance to do anything God said, "It is very good" (Gen 1:31 NRSV). Who we *are* is more foundational to our identity, more important in finding meaning in life, in knowing peace, than anything we can do.

Why should this be any different for God?

Newton's Law and God's Is

If it *were* true, that God really could just do *anything*, at any moment, cure every disease, give you back your lost job, allow you to make an "A" on that

---

8. This is a statement made to me by my friend, Dr. John Ballenger. The existential finality of this truth still haunts me.

exam you forgot to study for, make the sun stand still . . . then what? Once God intervened, even once, wouldn't all bets be off? Our infinite universe is so integrally connected that across the entire cosmos "for every action there is an equal and opposite reaction." Newton's third law of motion shows that if God were to step in, from outside of space and time, and pull a string just so things would fall my way, just this once, something, somewhere across the universe, is going to react. And what would that mean? If God grants a miraculous healing, what is the reaction? What does it do to gravitational attraction in our galaxy when God diverts the tornado from just one house because the inhabitants asked very politely? How does it affect the weak nuclear force when God throws that winning touchdown at the Superbowl?

I digress (and please pardon my sarcasm), but I hope you understand. Where would it end—if it ever began in the first place? Simply put, there is no way these essential, natural laws remain consistent if across the land, around the globe, in my own little world, God occasionally, randomly, capriciously injects divine intervention into the physical equation. If God ever chose just to do anything God pleased, the world as we know it would cease to be the world as we know it.

Of course, many people do maintain an interventionist theological perspective. That view is held by religious scholars whose IQs exceed mine. It just doesn't seem honest to me. Nor does it fit with the reality we know. We can choose to define God as omnipotent, and play all the consequent theological games, jump all the necessary (il)logical hoops, provide all the inevitably necessary qualifiers (but . . . if only . . . because . . . etc.), but this will only be necessary in order to defend a "Godness" *we* created from the beginning.

Maybe we should just say that we have been wrong.

We have the power and the right to redefine the theology we created so that it matches the reality we live. Bad things just happen to good people. *C'est la vie*. Where is God? What does God do?

God Is.

The "Intervention" of Presence

What more could God possibly do? What more could we expect or want God to do? God is around us, in people, in experiences, in the quiet, in our thoughts, our hearts, our souls. In our story of faith, told through the life of Jesus, the last word is, "I will be with you" (Rev 22:21 NRSV). In the good and the bad, through thick and thin, "through the valley of the shadow of death" (Ps 23:4 NRSV) and out the other side of that valley, God Is. With us. All around us. In us. But that presence is not physical intervention, the presence is love.

In a sense, to ask what God *does* is to misunderstand God. Our need for God to "do more" perhaps shows our insecurity, our immaturity, maybe our selfishness. "God, get down here and do more. For me!"

After one of the highly publicized, sadly familiar US episodes in which an unarmed African American man was shot by a white police officer, the Charlotte community gathered over successive summer Monday evenings to talk. There was a lot of talk in those meetings of what we could *do*, of not getting stuck in just talking. At the beginning of one of the sessions the facilitator addressed the concern and acknowledged our need to move to a different level of action, but he offered a word of important corrective. While not affirming apathy, he said something like "we need to remember that talking and doing are not diametric opposites. By talking, we *are* doing."

In his book *Wishful Thinking*, Frederick Buechner addresses this reality for both human and divine agency:

> In Hebrew the term *dabar* means both "word" and "deed." Thus, to say something is to do something. "I love you." "I hate you." "I forgive you." "I am afraid of you." Who knows what such words do, but whatever it is, it can never be undone. Something that lay hidden in the heart is irrevocably released through speech into time, is given substance and tossed like a stone into the pool of history, where the concentric rings lap out endlessly.
>
> Words are power. . . .
>
> In a sense I do not love you first and then speak it, but only by speaking it give it reality. "In the beginning was the Word," says John, meaning perhaps that before the beginning there was something like Silence. . . . Then the Word. The Deed. . . . "The Word was with God, and the Word was God," says John. By uttering [Godself], God makes God heard and makes God hearers. God never seems to weary of trying to get across to us.[9]

God speaks. This has been the universal declaration of people of faith through all times. Perhaps God has spoken audibly to some (or maybe not), but the more common experience is to hear the voice of God in nature and

9. Buechner, *Wishful Thinking*, 96.

experience, through the beauty of visual art and music and poetry, through the wisdom and voices of friends and fellow travelers, and perhaps most loudly, echoing in the silence that speaks to our souls through the "still small voice" (1 Kgs 19:12). God speaks. It is a deeply personal experience, an experience known, felt within the intimacy of one's own spirit. Who could deny this? What gives anyone the right to discredit someone else's experience? God speaks.

Many years ago, serving as an associate pastor, I was sitting in the hospital with a church member whose death was imminent. The family had called for the pastor, and I was as anxious for him to arrive as they were. He was well-known for pastoral care, having spent his whole career sitting long hours in waiting rooms, driving across town, even flying across the country to be with the members of his congregation. Extending care, especially in a time of crisis, was his specialty. As a young minister, I was excited to learn from the best. We waited.

When he arrived, the air cleared. I stepped back to take notes. The pastor, a former collegiate basketball player, was a presence in any room. His confidence matched his imposing physical frame. I was anxious to learn what to say in such a moment. As he entered the room, he offered a quiet word to members of the family surrounding the bed as he made his way to the far side. Pulling up a chair, he took a seat, and took the dying man's hand. There he remained, in that silent posture, until the man breathed his last.

Not a word was spoken. There was no miracle offered. No magic was conjured. There was nothing *done* at all, unless just being present counts—and my guess is that for this family, the quiet presence of their pastor, his quiet but large presence made all the difference.

It always does.

God is around us, speaking to us, being all that God is, in every good deed, every kind word, every growing experience, and in the powerful presence of each silent moment.

What more should we want God to do?

"I am that I am" (Exod 3:14 NRSV).

God. Always. **Does**. Everything. God. Can. Do.

5

God. Always. Does. **EVERYTHING.** God. Can. Do.
(God beside Us)

"If I ascend to heaven, you are there;
if I make my bed in Sheol, you are there." (Ps 139:8 NRSV)

God's not in Heaven and all's right on earth.
God is on earth, and all Hell's broke loose!

CLARENCE JORDAN[1]

1. "News, Views, Notes, and Quotes," para. 50.

Questions to Prompt Your Reading

How much control do we have over life/death, through medicine/technology? Is there a limit to what science should be able to do?

Can you identify an experience that signaled the "end of innocence" for you? Was it through an experience of education . . . death . . . sex . . .? As you think back about a time of naivete, what was good about it? What was harmful about it?

What kind of maturing experience have you had with God? With an understanding of faith?

Is fear a dynamic in your faith? Fear of the future? Fear of heaven and hell? Fear of God?

What is the relationship of power to fear, or fear to power?

When bad things happen to people, is there a reason? (Is there a connection between the tragedy and one's relationship with God?)

Does God punish us?

Are there coincidences in life? Is God at work in the coincidences in your life? What is the difference in coincidence and providence?

"We've Done Everything We Can Do"

My wife's father was in the hospital, one of those many episodes that accompany what may be a specifically American death. With each hospitalization the doctors had evaluated the patient, ordered a new battery of tests, mostly the same ones they had ordered the last time, and met with the family to pronounce a new strategy: the medications, the surgical options, the prognosis.

The last time, however, was different. It has to be. Even though we should know it is coming, no one is ever prepared for those terminally sobering words: "We've done everything we can do." My wife wasn't prepared for these words. As a pastor, she knows all the indications of death, and is trained and experienced in helping people hear this sentence, in giving comfort, in offering hope against hope. She wasn't listening that day as a pastor, however, and somehow the words she had heard dozens of times before rang differently in the ears of a daughter. If it weren't such a deathly serious subject, the dialogue would almost have been comical:

Doctor: "We've done everything we can do."

Daughter: "Thanks, doc. So, what's next? Where do we go from here?"

Doctor: "No, what I said is that there is nothing more we can do."

Daughter: "So what I hear you saying is that we'll have to go in a different direction from here, right? Try a new treatment. Is surgery an option?"

Doctor: "I said everything. We've done everything."

Daughter: "No. There's something more you can do. You've got to do something else. What else is there?"

Doctor: "We've done everything there is to do."

It's just that *everything* is not enough. Is it?
Even with God.
Technology and medical advances are unspeakable blessings. Life in an advanced twenty-first century society would not even be recognizable to most generations of human life. The incredible achievements of the last few centuries have rendered a life expectancy and a quality of life that are unmatched in human history. They also have created an illusion against reality. In truth, even with all this advancement we are no better than the ancients about talking about death, in preparing for its inevitability. In contrast to

our ancestors, we live with science, but since the existential questions are just as real today as they ever have been, we use our science as a protection against reality, idolatrizing healthcare, forcing the medical establishment to master the ultimately unsatisfactory goal of delaying death, prolonging death, avoiding death, and drawing out the "life" that leads to death. Death remains, and all our advance has led us no closer to an understanding or to providing any comfort with the reality.

A pastor once said to me that he reminds his parishioners in those difficult moments of life that "medicine only provides an illusion of control." We want doctors to have unlimited control, and, having been nurtured by such amazing healing and prolonging abilities, we are lured into a trap of believing they are unlimited. When we finally face the reality of the limitation of medicine, we experience another end of innocence, and that threshold is no easier to cross than any other of life's growing up moments.

If only we could grow up in our vision of God.

Growing Up and Doing without God

Could it be that we really have misunderstood God for all these long millennia? Could it be that what God really means, that what God really wants, that what God really *is* has to do with a similar growing up experience in life? Dietrich Bonhoeffer made this strange affirmation:

> Thus, our coming of age leads to a truer recognition of our situation before God. God would have us know that we must live as those who manage their lives without God. The same God who is with us is the God who forsakes us.[2]

Bonhoeffer recognized the infantile relationship we often have with the Divine. We have wrapped our understanding of the deity in sophisticated language and codified "God" through the doctrines and dogmas that result from millennia of theological discourse, but popular religion is replete with expressions of servile dependence on God. The religion that shields its adherents from the reality of suffering, while demanding more and more helpless dependence on the All-Powerful, is popular and persuasive—but it is a religion that too often crumbles in the face of life's storms. The fix-it God of such religious understanding represents the same type of thinking,

2. Bonhoeffer, *Letters and Papers*, 360.

perhaps the same emotional insecurity as we see in the family member who unrealistically expects the doctors to just make everything better.

Inherent to growing up is facing the reality of life and death. Facing the reality of God—the God who can't—ought to be inherent to maturing faith as well.

Unfortunately, theology misplaces its affirmations, piously defending God's omnipotence, while in reality failing to recognize God's omnipresence.[3] In other words, our theology has created a God who can do everything, anything, *when* God decides to show up and do it. But where does such a theology leave us? Even when we are not aware of it, such religion recommends for its followers a hopeless servility, a helpless dependence, and a childish faith,[4] when those qualities are nearly opposite of what good parents hope for their own children. We speak of "cutting the apron strings," raising children to be independent, self-sufficient, not perpetually dependent on daddy's money or mama's care. If God is "our Father" as Jesus suggested, why should that relationship be any different than that which we hope for in an earthly parent/child relationship?

Maybe God does, in fact, want us to come of age and manage our lives "without God"—not living without the presence of God, but without the illusion of the overweening control of God. That conceptualization of God, a God who watches like the proverbial "helicopter parent," can be debilitating. A good place to begin this maturing process is in replacing the need-based theology of omnipotence with a consistent theology of omnipresence. Let us explore that statement by considering what it would mean to affirm that God, in fact, always does *everything* God can do.

Relax in the Grace of God

The first thing we should say is that an affirmation of the omnipresence of God might allow theists, maybe especially Christian believers raised in a climate of evangelicalism, to relax in the grace of God. I used that phrase once, to the consternation of a friend who quickly reminded me that we cannot relax, for there is too much to keep us anxiously working, all the obligations to please and appease an angry/loving God. We cannot relax because there

---

3. While this book is an exploration of my understanding through Christian faith, my encounters with representatives of other religious traditions tell me the same dynamics are present in all the major religions.

4. This "childish" faith is not the same thing as the "childlike" faith Jesus commended.

is too much to fear: namely, as my friend said quite plainly: "Hell!" The basic spiritual posture of many believers is just that: fear, not trust.

Inherent in the meaning of the Greek word for faith (*pisteuo*), however, is a sense of abiding confidence or trust. This understanding of faith speaks of Jesus's understanding of God as an Abba, Father, one worthy of respect and trust. If power trumps presence as the defining attribute of God, it is understandable to approach God always looking over your shoulder, but that is not the image conveyed by Jesus's relationship to God. Do we trust in the goodness of God? The justice of God? The grace of God? If God is love, and our understanding of God leads us to love, then there can be no fear: "Perfect love casts out all fear" (1 John 4:18 NRSV).

A belief in omnipotence must lead to the logical conclusion that God is ultimately responsible for everything, the good and the bad. If God created out of nothing, then even the freedom of choice, even the opportunity to do evil, must be laid at the feet of the creator.[5] As it is usually understood, then, there is little alternative but to fear. Raw power always evokes fear, even when that fear parades as awe.

In the dawning of consciousness, humans became aware of the self, a movement of our evolution that still baffles and inspires science. That awareness led to or perhaps was inseparable from the dawning spiritual awareness of an "other," the neighbor, the enemy, and the "Other"—God. Since that affirming and threatening moment of realization, one of the persistent cries of faith has come in the moment of crisis. We hear this reflected in many of the experiences of the psalmists and the prophets of the Hebrew Scriptures: Where are you, God? "How long, O Lord?" (see Pss 13:1; 35:17; Hab 1:2; etc.) But why this despair? Why this lack of faith? Why this fearful, skeptical, trembling helplessness? The cry comes from looking for God as power, rather than seeing and seeking God as presence.

God is everywhere: in the good and the bad, in our successes and failures. In life's victories and our most bitter disappointments. In life's crises, rather than hoping God will get down here and do something, faith should give us the courage simply to know God is already, and always, here. Where else could God be? God is always doing not just something, but everything God can do! God was, before we arrived. God will be, after we are gone. We have no need to fear or beg or cajole.

5. See the discussion of creation "ex nihilo" in chapter 2.

Where Is Everywhere?

One of the most inspiring affirmations concerning the everywhere-presence of God comes from the psalmist's proclamation:

> Where can I go from your spirit? ·
> *Or where can I flee from your presence?*
> If I ascend to heaven, you are there;
> *if I make my bed in Sheol, you are there.*
> If I take the wings of the morning
> *and settle at the farthest limits of the sea,*
> even there your hand shall lead me,
> *and your right hand shall hold me fast.*
> If I say, "Surely the *darkness* shall cover me,
> *and the light around me become night,*"
> even the darkness is not dark to you;
> *the night is as bright as the day,*
> *for darkness is as light to you.* (Ps 139:7–12 NRSV; emphases added)

What a bold and ironic proclamation! In this passage the psalmist offers unconventional wisdom, a threefold challenge to the conventional wisdom of his day. The number three signified completeness according to Hebrew symbolism, so this text expresses the psalmist's emphatic claim: there is, literally, no where we can go to escape the presence of God.

First, in the ancient world Sheol defined the shadowy, Godless abode of the dead. The preacher of the book of Ecclesiastes says flatly, "Whatever your hand finds to do, do with your might; for there is no work or thought or knowledge or wisdom in Sheol, to which you are going" (Eccl 9:10 NRSV). No work, no thought, no knowledge, no wisdom—no God. Though an inaccurate translation, Sheol is sometimes called hell. Borrowing that mistranslation, however, might put the picture squarely in focus: even in hell we would not escape the presence of God! Could there be a greater paradox?

In the second place, the sea signified a place of fearful chaos in the ancient world. In creation, God summoned life from the "face of the deep," calling all life from the "darkness" (Gen 1:2). The prophet Isaiah depicts Yahweh as conquering "the dragon," one of the mythological monsters of the wild ocean, and controlling the waters, parting the sea so the Israelites can cross, escaping the pursuing Egyptians (Isa 51:9–10). With this ancient understanding of the sea as a place of mystery and fearful chaos, the miracle attributed to Jesus in all three synoptic gospels, the stilling of the storm[6] was an important means of connecting Jesus with the Divine. Only God can control the uncontrollable sea.

Finally, rounding out this trifecta of emphases, light and darkness have always been symbolic of the presence and the absence of goodness, the experience of, and the need for God. The biblical story says the first act of God was to separate light from darkness: "Let there be light" (Gen 1:1), and the soaring prologue of John's Gospel extends the work of God from literal light/darkness to its spiritual counterpart in the coming of Jesus: "The light shines in the darkness, and the darkness did not overcome it" (John 1:5 NRSV).

The psalmist's message is delivered with three-fold completeness, even in the least-expected places—the "godless" places, the chaotic places, the darkest places—God Is. God is everywhere.

What would it mean to the faith of fearful people if they could believe this affirmation, if they could be confident that in every situation, at all times, in all places, God was already there? What would it mean if no praying or pleading was needed to convince God to show up? I can think of no better word than confidence. If God were presence, perpetual, *everywhere* presence, wouldn't that instill confidence in our faith? God's presence could no longer be attributed to human achievement, or human righteousness, which is often little more than self-righteousness. God does not show up because we pray well or live rightly or give enough. God "shows up" because it is the nature of God never to leave in the first place. God is *everywhere*.

"Stuff" Happens to Good People, Sometimes There Is No Reason

Accepting that God is with us everywhere would invite Christians to grow up in their faith. If God is always with us, then life's difficulties are neither the result of human failure nor God's judgment. To quote the title of the book by Rabbi Kushner again, why do bad things happen to good people? The answer is a grown-up answer, one that is not easy for some people to hear or accept. The truth of the matter is that this is just life, what and how life is. Bad things happen to good people and to bad people alike, as Jesus knew: "God makes the sun rise on the evil and on the good and sends rain on the righteous and on the unrighteous" (Matt 5:45 NRSV). Or, to

6. See Matt 8, Mark 4, and Luke 8.

paraphrase Forrest Gump, "stuff happens!" A realistic understanding of life recognizes that unfairness and indiscriminate injustice are simply woven into the fabric of existence, and not just *human* existence. A mature faith gives confidence that we can live with this reality, because God is with us.

Rather than blaming humans for the bad that befalls them, which, on the one hand can create insecurity, and on the other can create disdain for religion, let us accept that bad things simply happen. It is a grown-up answer. Likewise, rather than blaming God for the bad that befalls us, creating fearful, cowering, timid weaklings, let us accept that bad things simply happen, and when those bad things happen, God is there. Sometimes there is no reason. Everything is not caused by some divine purpose. God is neither Grandfather Giver nor divine Judge, Jury, and Executioner, but God is with us, everywhere.

If this notion of God causes you to ask, "Then, why have faith?" or "Why pray?" it may be because you have been conditioned by and are locked-in to a theology of reward and punishment: If . . . then. Do this . . . get that. You certainly can find that theology within the Bible, there is no doubt, but a theology of unconditional love and the goodness of grace is also there. Go look for it! Reward/punishment is the strategy of power. It is the preferred worldview of systems of all kinds. It is not the message of Jesus, and the God who is always everywhere needs neither the carrot nor the stick to show up and be God.

God "shows up," because God is always with us. God Is. God is everywhere.

To accept that God *is* (chapter 1), that God is always *all* that God is (chapter 2), and that God's very nature is *action* (chapter 3) implies that if God is everywhere, always everywhere, then God will, obviously, always be doing everything that is in God's power to do. Omnipresence means God is working every angle. In the warp and woof of the total human reality, God is working.

With the random chance of the evolutionary process, God is working. In the natural processes, microscopic and macroscopic, which make the world turn, God is working. Through human relationships, God is working. By the technologies of advanced science, God is working. In the mystery that exceeds materialistic naturalism, mechanistic determinism, in those unexplainable events that are often called miraculous or supernatural, God is working. "God is the energy in all things, always working for the good" (Rom 8:28).

In all things, God is working!

To accept this theology, we will have to give up the personal God, that "Man Upstairs" who is called on by our fears and prayers to manipulate the events of this world in our favor, to bend natural laws for our isolated benefit—regardless of the effect that result may have on other people. Yes, we will lose that "God" in a new theology, but in its place we will gain an appreciation for Spirit and Mystery and Movement and Love.

Presence *is* work. If you do not believe that to be the case, you have never sat quietly with a loved one, silently doing "nothing," only attending to the grief of heartache or loss. On the other hand, if you have been on the receiving end of such a labor of love, you know there is nothing greater than the active power of silent presence.

A Thought Experiment: My Parents and My Cancer

Consider the following thought experiment as a kind of proof of this logic. Suppose I was diagnosed with a terminal cancer. God forbid, but what would happen? What would I hope for? What might I expect, especially, using this thought experiment, from my parents? They brought me into this world. I am, quite literally, created by them, in their image. They raised me, loved me, provided for me, and cared for me. Then they set me free. Through the complexity of genetic heritage, they may in fact be responsible for my hypothetical diagnosis. But what could they really do? Could they wave a magic wand and simply cure my cancer? No, they could not. Could they suspend the laws of nature and remove the mutation that initiated the tumor? No, they could not. Could they rewind time and reroute my destiny? No, they could not. No, all those supernatural qualities are simply out of their power. But, would their powerlessness over this situation make them useless to me? Powerless as my parents?

By no means!

What my parents *could* do, and what I know they *would* do, is to be present with me. They would call me. They would visit me. They would support me as I sought the advice of medical professionals. They would provide financial support to sustain my family. They would pray for me and ask their friends and church members to do likewise. They would be with me, even when they were not present with me, physically. Throughout the process, regardless of how deep and dark the valley I had to traverse, they would love me. In short, they would do everything, absolutely everything they could do for me.

If my disease were eliminated, medically or surgically, they would celebrate with me. If it disappeared, as on a very rare occasion diseases unexplainably do, they would rejoice. And, if the disease won that final battle, they would be heartbroken, but would still be with me, to grieve, and they would remain present for my family who survived my death. Everything. They would do everything they could. And I would know that at every turn, with every angle, in every single thing they would be there for me. But they could not cure me, because they simply do not have that power.

Now, as this thought experiment continues, let us ask the really hard question: would I *want* them to have this power? Think carefully before you answer.

The quick, easy answer, upon which too much theology is based, is yes, of course. I would want to be healed, so I would want them to have that power. But, think carefully about what that would mean, all the implications. What else would it mean, if my parents really did have the power to intervene within the natural process? What would that mean if they could subvert natural order and do, even once, what could not normally (naturally) be done? What would it do to my psyche, as a free child, a mature, responsible son of theirs, to know that at any moment they could pull down the foundations of the universe and change the immutable laws of nature, just for me? Or just against me.

You may still be answering yes, but consider the fact that I have a brother and a sister. Let us further hypothesize that each of them was also tragically diagnosed with a terminal disease. What if my parents chose to heal me, but I watched both of my siblings wither away and die long, agonizing deaths, even though my parents actually had the power to heal them? What would that mean to me? What would it mean to my siblings? What would it mean about my parents? Or, what if they chose to heal my sister and brother, and I watched my siblings enjoy the benefits of restored health and wholeness while I suffered and finally knew that there was to be no healing. What would that mean?

Isn't this precisely what we say of God and God's power?

Any parent who truly had the power to heal his or her child, but chose not to do so, would be considered ignorant or immoral or evil. What possible justification could be given for such negligent, if not heinous behavior? In his book *The Will of God,* Leslie Weatherhead says we should never excuse in God what we would otherwise criminalize in human behavior: "Surely we cannot identify as the will of God something for which a man would be locked up in jail or put in a criminal lunatic asylum."[7] This principle could serve as a simple test of the integrity of our own theology. In other words, any theology that justifies or rationalizes a negligent or criminal view of God should be rejected outright. An honest evaluation of the doctrine of omnipotence must recognize the way such a doctrine implicates God in the evil of this world. The scientific bent of our postmodern world prejudices many people against religion, all religion as hopelessly antiquated, tribal, and superstitious. Christians who wish to be taken seriously in that kind of world must not overlook this critique of omnipotence.

Furthermore, if God had such power to miraculously cure cancer on a divine whim, what would that really mean for our relationship with the Divine? Surely, we could not, in any real way, be truly free. The illusion of freedom, the illusion of a natural relationship to the world around us would be shattered with every divine healing.

God Is Omnipotent: The Games We Play

One way to maintain the doctrine of omnipotence in the face of this contradiction is to claim that God truly is all-powerful, but to mitigate this claim by allowing that at the beginning of time, out of God's own wisdom and will, God constrained God's own power. This admission would allow us to affirm that God, technically, possesses unlimited power, while recognizing that the use of such power, even once, would cause the universe to cease to be the world as we know it. Some thoughtful Christians maintain such a view despite the obvious fact, which they admit, that all the laws of nature would have to be thrown out the window if God monkeyed with them, even once. Such an affirmation is logically redundant, spiritually unnecessary, and is one that limits human and divine agency, becoming dangerous in its full implication.

This kind of explanation only becomes logically necessary after the fact, i.e., in order to defend a definition of God which includes omnipotence—but whose definition of "Godness" is that to begin with? Where did it come from? Why? Theology is a human construct, a system of human words designed to create conceivable images of the Divine. Doctrines are words that seek to describe our experience of and relationship with that

7. Weatherhead, *Will of God*, 12–13.

great Mystery. The purpose of this humanly created theological language is to deepen one's personal identity and to improve one's life and social relationships, and to enhance our engagement with the world around us.

I believe a doctrine of omnipotence fails those aims. The "theology of reality" I am advocating will demand that we employ the best of human wisdom, and such wisdom will embolden us to admit the uncertainty of life, while not requiring us to renounce the reality of God. The very real experience of the Divine will not permit us to make that mistake.

Affirming God's existence in all things, and God's relationship with all things, will permit modern Christians to maintain a confession of faith *and* accept the findings of modern science. God does not simply stand beyond the natural realm, controlling all things by divine whim. God stands beside us, walking with us along every journey. Being all that God is, always, God never ceases to be (which means to *do*) all we should expect—which should be all we need.

"If I ascend to heaven, you are there; if I make my bed in Sheol, you are there."

God. Always. Does. **EVERYTHING.** God. Can. Do.

AN ASIDE: MIRACLES

Much like prayer, which is a kind of "rubber meets the road" proof of divine power and good faith, a miracle is said to serve the same function: proving God's omnipotent power, and, as an added benefit, providing exactly what the faithful believer wants! Naming and claiming your miracle is fodder for ecstatic, faith-healing crusades, but also for many Sunday sermons and even the daily prayers of the faithful.

Miracles are the focus of the Bible's best stories, and nothing seems too outlandish: an axe head floats, a donkey talks, the sea is parted, the lame, the blind, the deaf are healed with a word, even the dead are raised. In the biblical world, there's a certain logic in those stories that does not hold in a twenty-first-century world. In a world which understood that the weather and the waves, all drought and disease and death, were held in the hands of God, used at the direction of the Almighty, it's hardly unreasonable to say God caused the sun to stand still in the sky.

But the sun does not move across the sky! That's just an illusion. For the sun to remain stationary, the earth would have to stop spinning. Without that rotation, life as we know it would cease. That "miracle" cannot be. It's not that it cannot be a miracle, it is that the actions described could never happen (and anyone live to tell it). Science proves this.

So, *does* God intervene, interrupting the laws of nature to achieve the divine will? Modern Christians need to think carefully about that question.

My friend, the late Dr. William E. Hull, once said, "A miracle is not the contradiction of natural law by supernatural law, but the contravention of one natural law by another, yet unknown, natural law." Dr. Hull understood that any event which interrupted one natural law, interwoven with all other laws, spelled the end of the world as we know it. It is true that in ages past, many events interpreted as miracle have been shown to be only the work of a yet-understood law. The thousand-year flood is not God's wrath. It is meteorology, geology, and physics.

Yet one could argue that Dr. Hull's definition, in fact, eliminates God. If all divine action will one day be proven to be only a natural law, is there room for God? This is the "God of the gaps" argument: each new scientific insight pushes God further out of the picture, until we finally can explain everything without God. Defining miracle as it is commonly understood runs this risk. Nature-contradicting interventions do not, cannot occur. Christians need to understand why this is so. But to limit God to the gaps of our understanding is to set the bar too low.

Is God supernatural? If that definition places God separate from nature, able to intervene on a whim, we must reject that idea. And if supernatural means God is just some part of the natural world, the superlative force of nature itself, we also must reject that. God is more than all of that, and if that sounds unbelievable, it should. We're talking about *God!*

God works within, and yet beyond nature, not contradicting its laws but contravening with a different presence altogether. Biblical miracles proved, from the writer's perspective, God's activity in the world. They were theological affirmations, not scientific observations. They were events that opened the eyes of the people, turning them to God. The event, always viewed in retrospect, changed things—so miracles do happen, still, because real life events still bring people to see God. And seeing God is not a matter for scientific exploration. It is a matter of the heart. What could be more important?

People saw and interpreted biblical events within their frame of understanding. We do the same. How could it be otherwise? As our understandings of the world and God change, the way we understand miracle will also change. What will not change is God—"the energy in all things, always working for the good" (Rom 8:28). As people experience that energy, and they will in every age, there will always be the need for a word to explain it. Let's call it a miracle.

6

God. Always. Does. Everything. **GOD.** Can. Do. (God with Us)

"When you pass through the waters, I will be with you. . . . because . . . I love you." (Isa 43:2, 4 NRSV)

Someday after mastering the winds, the waves, tides and gravity . . . we shall harness for God the energies of love and for the second time in the history of the world [humanity] will discover fire.

TEILHARD DE CHARDIN[1]

---

1. Teilhard de Chardin, "Harnessing the Energies of Love."

Questions to Prompt Your Reading

What was the first Bible verse you learned?

Does God allow bad things to happen, meaning God *could* stop them but chooses not to do so?

What bad things do parents allow to happen to their children?

It is one thing to say parents allow children to learn from the school of hard knocks (skinned knees, stubbed toes, etc.), but what would it say if a parent allowed their child to die if the parent could have prevented that death?

If someone loves, does that make the person strong or show a streak of weakness?

If it is true that "God is love" (1 John 4:8 NRSV), what strength might be implied by those words?

If God is true love, what limitations might be implied by those words?

God Is Love (All We Need to Know)

Deeper than the deepest ocean, higher than the farthest star, more intricate than the tiniest snowflake, purer than a child's delight, it is the subject of the greatest art, inspiration of the greatest music, and source of the most passionate poetry. More pursued than the rarest gem, and more elusive, kings can't buy it, yet it is free for the taking to any peasant who will give his or her heart to it. It is a "many-splendored thing."[2] It makes the world go around. It never dies. It's what God is.

God is love.

This book starts, stops, and is saturated with those three words, which are undoubtedly the first biblical words most of us who grew up in the shadow of the church ever learned: "God is love" (1 John 4:8 NRSV). It's too bad most of us could not have just stopped there. What more needs to be said? In 1988 a minister named Robert Fulghum penned one of the greatest book titles: *All I Really Need to Know I Learned in Kindergarten*. While adults certainly need a grown-up faith, the nuggets of fairness and honesty and cooperation that we learned from our first teachers in school and Sunday school often get obscured by life's complexities. So, too, with love.

In large measure this book is an effort to strip away some of those complexities from our conceptualizations about God. If we could teach kindergartners that they could really believe their first Bible lesson, we would have taught them all they need to know about God. Of course, there is more to "God is love" than a kindergartner, or even a full-grown adult, can understand. Love is our most complex emotion, its dynamics are multifaceted, but it is the place where our theology should begin. It is the place our theology must also end.

Justifying a Criminal God

All that can be said of God should begin here, and any attributes assigned to God, any claims made for God, any theologies postulated to define God that cannot easily conform to love as the central and defining characteristic of God's nature should be dismissed. Leslie Weatherhead's claim that I referred to in the previous chapter might seem obvious: anything that is illegal in human behavior should not be legitimized for God. This remarkable

2. *A Many-Splendored Thing* was a 1952 novel by Han Suyin. The book became a 1955 film and then a popular song, which was released by a number of different artists.

assertion refers to his rejection of a theology of substitutionary atonement as it is traditionally understood. He believes there is a better way to understand the death of Jesus than to say, "God sent Jesus *for the purpose* of dying." Such an action would be a criminal offense in human behavior, so how is it that such a heinous claim has become central to Christian theological understanding for so many, and a purported justification of God's so-called love?

Weatherhead was a pastor in London during the Second World War. He wrote in the heat of that conflict, which was devouring families and faith. Weekly, he was called to deliver sermons to mothers and fathers who had been broken by the tragic deaths of sons and daughters, whose faith was being tried by all the innocent lives lost in bombing raids. In this cauldron of emotional turmoil, he was being asked to defend and define, to provide theological justifications for such gripping loss. How could anyone possibly look into all those bloodred eyes, wrecked lives, and shattered souls and say God did this?

Let us be clear that this *is* what the orthodox answer means. If God *could* have stopped any of those senseless deaths, which would have kept so many from walking away from sane lives and life-giving faith, but chose not to do so, for any reason, if God simply *chose* not to do so, wasn't God (who created out of nothing and made all the rules[3]) responsible for such grief and apostasy? Neglect of those in your care is a crime in American jurisprudence just as much as intentional malice is, yet somehow we have twisted this negligence, when attributed to God, sadly warping it into a defense of divine love.

Not too long ago I read the following unfortunate submission on Facebook:

> I've been a deep believer my whole life. 18 years as a Southern Baptist. More than 40 years as a mainline Protestant. I'm an ordained pastor. But it's just stopped making sense to me. You see people doing terrible things in the name of religion, and you think: "Those people believe just as strongly as I do. They're just as convinced as I am." And it just doesn't make sense anymore. It doesn't make sense to believe in a God that dabbles in people's lives. If a plane crashes, and one person survives, everyone thanks God. They say, "God had a purpose for that person. God saved her for a reason." Do we not realize how cruel it is to say that if God had a purpose for that person, [God] also had a purpose for killing everyone else on that

3. See the discussion of creation "ex nihilo" in chapter 2.

plane? And a purpose in starving millions of children? A purpose in slavery and genocide? For every time you say that there's a purpose behind one person's success, you invalidate billions of people. You say there is a purpose to their suffering. And that's just cruel.[4]

I responded to this post:

What if we, human beings, have just radically misunderstood "God" for a very long time? What if God isn't most intrinsically "power" (the One, or the Force that makes things happen or not, which does make God responsible for a lot of bad stuff). . . . What if God actually is what Scripture taught us at our most impressionable age: God is love.

Wouldn't that change everything, from fighting wars in God's name to having "believers" leave their faith because such a God just (understandably) quit making sense? Wouldn't that change EVERYTHING? Maybe God IS love. Just love.

Think of so many other unfortunate things you have heard someone say about God, atrocious claims made by widely quoted pastors and Christian leaders: AIDS as God's punishment for the homosexual, natural disasters and 9/11 as our nation's punishment for lapsed morals, etc. A child dies, and no matter the cause, cancer, abuse, an automobile accident, someone says, "It was God's will" or "Everything happens for a reason" or "When we get to heaven, this will make sense." But how could we ever justify such unrelenting, purposeless pain as the will of a loving God? Could you imagine suggesting that any of those fates were the will of that child's parents? Of course not, yet we have been taught to say, blithely, it was God's will. It certainly is not the will of love!

Love does know this kind of pain. Love does suffer such devastating loss—so love is uniquely positioned to help us endure—but love is never its cause.

Claims such as these, horrendous as they are, *can* be made of a God of power, but if the heart of the Divine is pure love, these simply cannot be said to be the purpose or the provision of God. The God of love *allowed* the Holocaust, because of free will? Really? Because God consented to a kind of tough love that parents sometimes have to offer, in order to teach their children? Really? Do you know a single mother, a sane, emotionally stable mother, who would allow the senseless death of even one of her children, just for the sake of tough love—much less six million of them!?

4. "I've Been a Deep Believer."

What self-respecting father would go to such ghastly lengths to show his superiority? Only a God whose defining nature is brute force, a God bent on defending that power at any expense, could make such an absurd claim.

"God is love."

Napoleon allegedly claimed,

> Alexander, Caesar, Charlemagne, and myself have founded empires. But upon what did we rest the creations of our genius? Upon force. Jesus Christ alone founded his empire upon love; and at this hour millions of men would die for him.[5]

Napoleon recognized the power of love, and presumably the transience of force, yet the seductive lure of raw power was irresistible to his ego, as it is to most of us. The spoils go to the fastest, the strongest, the first, no matter how brutal those winners may be, and though the power of love is undeniable, love is often reduced, ridiculed as a trait of weakness. Love is caricatured by sentimental niceties and the laughable foibles of the lovable loser. Love is often displayed as the Achilles heel, the tragic flaw, the ultimate downfall of the erstwhile hero. The love of power often seems to trump the power of love, even though anyone who has been ensnared in the powerful tentacles of love knows brute force is no match. "The greatest of these," the very greatest power there is, is love (1 Cor 13:13 NRSV).

Paradox: Omnipotence and the Greatest Power in the World

Herein lies the great problem and paradox of our language: if God is *love*, then God *is* (in essence, in the very heart of God's nature) the greatest power the world has ever known. Regarding the things that matter, ultimately in all that is essential to our humanity, what can love not accomplish? What divisions can it not repair? What wounds can it not heal? What goal can love not attain? Love is, in the most important way, all-powerful.

But all-powerful love cannot be the same thing as omnipotent force.

Martin Luther King Jr. said it well: "Darkness cannot drive out darkness: only light can do that. Hate cannot drive out hate: only love can do that."[6] When we strip away the vain egos, whose hard driving aim is the creation of bigger kingdoms centered around those egos, we find how weak power-as-brute-force really is. A domineering spouse can manipulate a

5. Jackson, "Origin of Christianity," para. 32.
6. King, *Strength to Love*, 47.

partner, holding together a facade of relationship, but no true marriage, which is a relationship of mutual benefit and satisfaction, has ever been built on coercion and control, on the destructive tools of fear and deception.

Nations have been built by the sword, maintained by militaries and policies of exploitation, and nationalistic pride has upheld mythologies of greatness. The Pax Romana, that national mythology of the ancient Roman Empire, comes to mind, but the warnings of the prophets Jeremiah and Ezekiel are instructive: trust no one who says, "Peace, peace, when there is no peace" (Jer 6:14; 8:11; Ezek 13:10 NRSV). Rome maintained its peace by creating in its subjects an uneasy fear, at best. At worst, Rome's so-called peace was just the desperate resolve of the oppressed masses, determined to cling to life. One day humanity will learn to judge greatness by attributes more important than armies and territories, conquests and repression. Hubert Humphrey said it right:

> The moral test of government is how that government treats those who are in the dawn of life, the children; those who are in the twilight of life, the elderly; and those who are in the shadows of life, the sick, the needy and the handicapped.[7]

To say it in the words of Jesus: "the least of these" (Matt 25:40 NRSV). Power cares for those in power. Love cares for those who cannot care for themselves, and love respects all.

Power may create a people, but it will never make the person. Power may amass and control bodies, but even when those bodies are enchained, enslaved, brute force cannot keep the human spirit from soaring. Human beings are soulful, thoughtful, spirited beings. We are more defined by our interior attributes than any external veneer. Only by touching and inspiring that intrinsic, inner nature do we ever truly reach the human person. Any effort to manipulate or control that spiritual nature[8] belies the selfish motivation of any such controlling force.

Power constrains; love sets free. Power fears; love trusts. Power is myopic; love is visionary. Power is restricted to physical means; love, motivated by human inspiration, not human agendas and aspirations, is open to

7. Alker, "Children," para. 1.

8. The use of the term "spiritual" is not synonymous with "religious" in this context. I do not refer to the human soul as some might consider the biblical image. I simply believe there is more to being a human being than our physical makeup. There is mind, not just brain. There is spirit, not just body. Human bodies can be constrained, but the human spirit cannot.

the sky. Power idolizes past accomplishments; love envisions future definitions of greatness. Power is about ego; love knows the benefit to the self is
contained within the benefit to the other.

If this sounds to you like the idealistic mumbo jumbo of an almost
pacifist pastor, please reconsider. Such a judgment could only be based on
a false understanding of love as weak sentimentality. Consider the words
of the apostle Paul to the church in Rome, as he quotes the wisdom of an
ancient sage, recorded in Prov 25:

> Let love be genuine; hate what is evil, hold fast to what is good; love
> one another with mutual affection; outdo one another in show-
> ing honor. Do not lag in zeal, be ardent in spirit, serve the Lord.
> Rejoice in hope, be patient in suffering, persevere in prayer. Con-
> tribute to the needs of the saints; extend hospitality to strangers.
>
> Bless those who persecute you; bless and do not curse them.
> Rejoice with those who rejoice, weep with those who weep. Live in
> harmony with one another; do not be haughty, but associate with
> the lowly; do not claim to be wiser than you are. Do not repay
> anyone evil for evil, but take thought for what is noble in the sight
> of all. If it is possible, so far as it depends on you, live peaceably
> with all. Beloved, never avenge yourselves, but leave room for the
> wrath of God; for it is written, "Vengeance is mine, I will repay,
> says the Lord." No, "if your enemies are hungry, feed them; if they
> are thirsty, give them something to drink; for by doing this you
> will heap burning coals on their heads."[9] Do not be overcome by
> evil, but overcome evil with good. (Rom 12:9–21 NRSV)

The rare instances in our human history when someone has actually held to Paul's high standard, has truly lived the power of love, those
instances will stand out in our history books perhaps as long as humans
endure—and these examples will not be remembered as caricatures of foolishness. Those intrepid few who have dared "not to be overcome by evil,
but to overcome evil with good" are hardly exemplars of flawed weakness.
Their rare actions of bold courage may be our highest expressions of the
true power of the human spirit.

9. Prov 25.21-22

Love and "Passyfism"

When Mahatma Ghandi, clad only in a robe and sandals, faced down Great Britain's imperial power, meeting that colonizing giant at its full strength, but armed only with words of truth, it was not weakness that was revealed. When Martin Luther King Jr. led thousands of voiceless Americans, dehumanized and disempowered by the evil of American racism, and those who were supposedly powerless stood up to terrifying threats and real, physical violence, fire hoses and dogs and humiliations and tauntings and beatings and lynchings, those gatherings were not the assemblies of the timid. Civil rights did not succeed as a movement of weakness. One student, unarmed and alone, standing before a Chinese tank in that now-iconic Tiananmen Square might be the perfect image of the true power: powerless truth exposing the cowardly power of brute force. When Jesus died at the hands of the Romans and dared to say of his brutal executioners: "Father, forgive them; for they do not know what they are doing" (Luke 23:34 NRSV), it is hardly an image of weakness that comes to mind.

Love is hardly what some have derided as "passyfism." Blessing those who persecute you is not recommended for the weak at heart, and overcoming evil with good still requires one to overcome evil! Often, the exemplars of love-as-true-power have paid the price for exposing the cowardly power of brute force, which always lashes out when exposed. It comes as no surprise that Ghandi, King, and Jesus were all killed.

On the other hand, the use of brute force can be a means of hiding behind one's weaknesses and fears. Gun violence, for example, may be a cowardly way out. The one using this powerful tool of violence never has to truly face her/his opponents hand to hand, eye to eye, man to man as the macho expression has it. Shooting someone at a distance is far easier than having a conversation. Letting a weapon do the talking is an easier, quicker fix, but in that "answer," the problem is never resolved, so it is certainly a less lasting resolution than one based on dialogue. When someone resorts to solving their issues with a gun, the real power is the weapon, not the one who uses it.

Dialogue, predicated on love, exposes honest feelings, and suggests compromise and a more thorough truce, and the relationship created by the dialogue is the only means to real peace. The old adage, often attributed to Gandhi, says, "An eye for an eye makes the whole world blind."[10] Weapons

10. Yadav, "Eye for an Eye."

and power will never lead to a world of light and sight. They are too weak a means for so grand an ideal.

In 2012, Libertarian candidate for the presidency, Ron Paul, identified this truth. In a debate sponsored by Fox News, Paul recommended a foreign policy based on the Golden Rule:

> If another country does to us what we do to others, we're not going to like it very much. So, I would say that maybe we ought to consider a golden rule in foreign policy. Don't do to other nations . . . what we don't want to have them do to us.[11]

What a brilliant suggestion, to use the Golden Rule, which is expressed in some form in all the world's major religions, as a guide for foreign policy and diplomacy. How could that fail? Ron Paul's suggestion wasn't "passy-fism." It wasn't even pacifism. He did not suggest disbanding the military, defunding the police, or emptying the budget of the Pentagon, but he did suggest letting common sense and a spirit of good will be the measure of our national policy.

The candidate made his comment in front of what may have been the nation's most purportedly Christian electorate. South Carolinians, especially the state's vocal Republicans, had positioned themselves as the nation's moral voice in that election, yet how did they respond to Ron Paul's biblical recommendation? When another candidate asked rhetorically what we should do to our enemies, and answered his own question "kill them," cheers rang through the auditorium. When a Libertarian politician dared to quote Jesus, South Carolina's *Christian* electorate rained down a chorus of boos on the candidate, as if to say: "Down with love, give us a national policy of power, no matter what Jesus says!"

Can you imagine the power that would come to a nation which dared to employ such a courageous plan of action? The nation would not need to empty its arsenal, but when would it ever need to employ bombs, drones, tanks, armed battalions, if it truly operated from a courageous position of honesty and justice with good will? "Doing unto others" (Matt 7:12 NRSV) would hardly be a platform of weakness. The very fact that no one, even the world's most powerful nation, has ever been willing to stand on such a platform may indicate that we are not yet strong enough, courageous enough, bold enough, truly powerful enough, to even make such an attempt.

---

11. Adams, "South Carolina Primary Race," para. 24.

My purpose here is not to engage in partisan politics. Love will always challenge all systems and institutions, and all political parties. There may be as many Democrats, Independents, and Ron Paul's own Libertarians who would reject a national policy based on biblical wisdom and the self-sacrificial example of Jesus as South Carolina's Republicans did. My purpose in citing this example is only to argue that I believe the power of love *could* be practiced as policy. That practice would hardly be mild mannered timidity or an invitation to self-assured destruction.

Love is not an invitation to become a doormat, to be walked over, taken advantage of, abused. Neither does love mean always getting what I want, when I want it. It does not mean holding the power to control every situation, and every person in every situation.

There are limits to what love can do. Everyone knows this from experience. There are some things I simply cannot do for my children, no matter who I am, no matter how much money or social or political power I possess, no matter how much I want to help, no matter how much I try to assist, no matter how much I feel I need to intervene. Love is a different kind of power altogether. Love is non-controlling power, non-manipulating power, self-giving power. Love accepts the conditions it has been given, lives into its own context, and creates outcomes we could never have imagined despite its inability to control any given context.

The Limits of Love and the Death of Jesus

If Christians took more seriously the incarnation of Jesus, and all that such a bold theology implies, perhaps we would not find the concept of a loving-and-therefore-limited God so difficult. The centerpiece of our theology is the death of Jesus. The cross is often misunderstood, and the unfortunate theologies born of a too-bloody atonement have been synonymous with Christianity for many Christians, yet, the death of Jesus *is* clearly the defining event of his life, the event through which his life's meaning is understood. His was a life of unwavering commitment, of sacrificial living. Rather than fight the leaders of the Jewish religious establishment in Jerusalem or incite a revolution to overthrow the oppressive power of Rome, Jesus was executed as a criminal of the state. In time this humiliating death was reinterpreted within a developing theological framework, not as a defeat, the indication of ultimate weakness in the face of Roman and religious power, but as God's power—the power of self-sacrificial love. What the Romans intended for evil, God used for good (to paraphrase Gen 50:20).

Jesus's death was not the plan of God, if that means God's beforehand intention. Wouldn't that be a criminal offense? The intended and unintended consequences that befall a fallen world led to the death of Jesus. Through the power of love God used that unintended outcome for a more powerful end. Jesus's death carries a message of forgiveness, encourages a life of sacrificial generosity, symbolizes self-giving love, and that message has now been carried to the whole world. Think how much more powerful that message is, understood correctly, than the story of just one more underdog, beating the odds and trumping the power that had sought to destroy it.

The problem with that theology is that we cannot leave it alone, cannot accept it at face value. We cannot let it be what it is and what it needs to be, namely, a theology intrinsically based in love. Ironically, as it came to be interpreted, and is largely understood, it is a theology couched in love—but love only as a thin cover for redemptive violence, which is a theology based on power. An old gospel song, based on the text of Matt 26:53, twists this theology of love, reframing the death of Jesus within the context of the power, the brute force of God. "He could have called ten thousand angels to destroy the world and set him free. He could have called ten thousand angels, but he died alone for you and me."[12]

Could Jesus have called ten thousand angels, really? Maybe the more important question is this: if he *could* have, if he had truly possessed some kind of supernatural, interrupt-the-laws-of-nature intervening power, could that kind of death really be called sacrificial?

If I am in complete control, if I know that anything I lose today is not actually lost, if I know I'll just get it back tomorrow, is that really sacrifice? Wouldn't that, in any real terms, just be a facade of sacrifice, a kind of game, perhaps used to manipulate or toy with the ones held under my power? Does not true *sacrifice* require an actual loss of whatever power one had to begin with? Doesn't sacrifice mean a genuine relinquishment of control, a truly costly action offered in the face of true uncertainty, with a sure sense of impending loss? How could anything less than that be called sacrifice? If it does not cost you anything, can it truly be called love? What love is there that knows no sacrifice?

"God is love."

12. Griffin, "Story Behind the Song," para. 1.

Who Wants a Weak God?

No one, it seems, wants a weak God, so rather than follow the theology that naturally flows from Jesus's life of self-sacrifice, we have created safeguards. We have created them intuitively, reflexively, and defensively to guard against such weakness. Ironically, in doing so we have logically destroyed the most powerful aspect of Jesus's incarnation, if only by implication. It is our great loss. Sacrifice that is in reality just a pretty storefront, a defensive facade to protect power as the supreme value is no sacrifice at all. Having created a God in our image, however, in the lustful need for power and control, we have had no recourse but to defend this "Godness" with our theologies, no matter how illogical or contradictory they may be.

If we believe in the power of love, what have we to fear? Jesus's living/dying example exemplifies a God who is love, and surely this God is more truly powerful than all the other gods, of all the other religions, living and dead, whose ultimate nature is brute force.

Learning to live with the acknowledgement and reality of our ultimate powerlessness—learning that I am not in control—is one of the maturing lessons of growing up. We need to take this step in our maturing understanding of the power of God. God is not in control, either, in the ways most of us were taught. This should be good news to all of us who have framed our worldview, centered the convictions of our faith, in a gift of unconditional, sacrificial love, rather than raw power.

The thirteenth chapter of Paul's first letter to the church at Corinth has been called the "Love Chapter." If God really is love, it may be helpful to learn to read those words anew:

> [God] is patient; [God] is kind; [God] is not envious or boastful or arrogant or rude. [God] does not insist on [God's] own way; [God] is not irritable or resentful; [God] does not rejoice in wrongdoing, but rejoices in the truth. [God] bears all things, believes all things, hopes all things, endures all things.
>
> [God] never ends. . . . Faith, hope, and [God] abide, these three; and the greatest of these is [God]. (1 Cor 13:4–13 NRSV)

If God bears all things, hopes all things, and endures all things, if God never ends—*never ends*—what more power could we ever need, in this life or the next?

God is that power, and that power is with us through thick or thin, good or bad, in the bitter and the sweet. The power of love, which has the power to change the world, not by magically changing our circumstances, but by transforming us one heart at a time, is a greater power than force or manipulation. Growing to accept and affirm that God is precisely that love, and nothing else, will change us. But not before remaking God.

Love is the power of the God who *can't*, and that God is always with us, and that love will always be enough—and that love is always with us, and that God will always be enough!

"When you pass through the waters, I will be with you . . . because . . . I love you" (Isa 43:2 NRSV). That love changes everything.

Love changes our perception of God, our relatedness to God, our relationship with God. Love changes our powerlessness in the face of disappointment and disillusionment. Love changes the potential of all human relationships. Love even changes our theology, teaching me, even in the course of writing this book, to say it differently from here to the end:

God. Always. Does. Everything. *LOVE*. Can. Do.

AN ASIDE: GOD

Who is God?[1]

It's a big question. Who *is* God? *What* is God? Many people who say they believe in God may never have really thought about God in this detailed way, may not have really asked about the nature, the substance, the ontology (the being-ness or essence) of God.

Maybe that's part of our problem.

As children, we are taught to believe in God from Sunday school lessons, from what we can glean from adult sermons, from the best efforts of parents and teachers. We also learn from the world around us, the hearsay of friends, popular books and movies, the culture at large. In all of this, our little brains inevitably seize on the concrete images which are presented. The Bible itself is full of concrete images: God as Creator, King, Warrior, Judge, Father, and these all rest comfortably alongside the cultural ideas, such as Father Time, the Man Upstairs, the Supernatural Being.

Since children's brains do not process abstract ideas, these images, which may or may not have been intended to convey anything nearly so concrete, the images inevitably lodge within our formative psyches. For many people, even if they have had extensive educational opportunity and life experience, those concrete images of childhood become permanent monuments. The images, in a practical way, *become* God.

One feature, common to many popular images, is that, in one way or another, these images all center around the characteristic of power. God is the Being who is defined by his power. (The Almighty is almost universally thought of in stereotypically masculine terms.) The word God essentially means power: power to create, power to control, power to win, to persuade,

1. Thousands of books have been written on this subject. I recommend: Harold Kushner, *When Children Ask about God*; Rob Bell, *What We Talk about*; Kirby Godsey, *When We Talk about God, Let's Be Honest*; Karen Armstrong, *The Case for God*.

to protect, power to change or to defeat. God is the power over all other powers.

But, what if this is not God at all? (After all, those qualities do sound a bit *human*, don't they?)

What if God is even bigger than power?

What if God is not even a Being, but something altogether more mysterious? What if God is entirely beyond that? A Supreme Being is a big idea, but we can all begin to conceptualize a Being who is like us, only an infinitely better version of us. What if, instead, God truly is incomprehensible?

Karen Armstrong, the British scholar of comparative religions, says, "God is not a being at all."[2] Her words echo one of the great theologians of the twentieth century, Paul Tillich, who spoke of God not as a Being, but as "the ground of Being-itself."[3] If this does not make sense, maybe it is not supposed to make sense, as Augustine said, "If you understand, it is not God."[4] This incomprehensibility of God led Tillich to acknowledge that the best of our understanding was the "God," essentially created from *our* images. True God must be the "God above God."

The thought of God totally beyond even our vaguest conception may be profoundly unsettling, but creating images of God may be mostly about control, *our* ability to control God—as we have defined God—for our own benefit. And this just brings us back to . . . power.

Maybe only an unknowable Presence, beyond being, beyond power, could truly be God.

2. Armstrong, *Case for God*, ix.
3. "God as Ground of Being," para. 1.
4. Amanor, "If You Understand," para. 1.

7

God. Always. Does. Everything. Love. CAN. Do. (God behind Us)

"My power is made perfect in weakness." (2 Cor 12:9 NRSV)

So perhaps we are beginning to get a little sense of what the real secret is in this Gospel. The secret is that the event which will change everything, which will bring in the regime of God, which will forgive sins and release people from guilt and fear, is not an event brought about by naked power. The God who is going to change everything, change forever the conditions in which human beings live, is a God who is "beyond" power as we would like to understand it; a God who does not coerce belief or clinch arguments, but who repeatedly demands relation and trust. This is the secret that Mark's Jesus wants to disclose—and it is, in the nature of the case, formidably difficult to disclose.

ROWAN WILLIAMS[1]

1. Williams, *Meeting God in Mark*, 238.

Questions to Prompt Your Reading

"God always does everything God can do." Does this statement give you pause? Why or why not?

If there were some things God literally *could not* do, how would this affect your understanding of divinity? Your relationship with God? Could this kind of deity even be God for you?

Would a God who was not able to do anything, literally, anywhere, anytime, be an *impotent* God, a powerless deity? What might a God, limited in ultimate power, be able to do?

Is the essence of God's nature power or love?

Are the power and the love of God in tension?

Have you experienced God truly being all-powerful? (Has every prayer been answered? Every trouble averted?) Have you ever said, "If *I* were God, I would have . . . stopped that . . . healed that . . . changed that. . . ?" How do you deal with the tension of believing in a God of love and a God of all power when there is so much sadness and evil in the world?

Do you ever feel the language of faith does not match your experience of the reality of pain and brokenness in this world?

Ay, There's the Rub!

To die—to sleep.
To sleep—perchance to dream: ay, there's the rub!
For in that sleep of death what dreams may come
When we have shuffled off this mortal coil,
Must give us pause.[2]

As Shakespeare's Hamlet contemplates his own suicide, he puts words to a sentiment we have all felt: conflict, tension, difficulty, i.e, "the rub." Had Frank Tupper said that day in Systematic Theology, "God always does everything God *wants* to do," or "God always does everything *we deserve* to have done," or "God always does everything God *chooses* to do," I would have had no issue, but what I heard Dr. Tupper say that day is, "God always does everything God *can* do." Ay . . . there's the rub!

Dr. Tupper affirmed this declaration the last time we spoke, several years before his death, though he said he had modified his statement. At that time, he told me he preferred to say, "God always does the most God can do—given the specificity of each context." I am sure this is not what he said twenty-five years ago, because I likely would not have flinched over that statement, if I had understood it at all.

Having been thoroughly trained in the school of the all-powerful God, I would have heard "the most God can do" as an affirmation of God's limitless power to affect and control within the context of God's omniscient providential care. In other words, I would have heard that though God *can* do anything and everything, there are times God chooses not to act. This may be for our own good, and we just don't know it. Or maybe God's inaction is an expression of "tough love." Or maybe there is a bigger picture that we can't see, even if the immediate picture involves tremendous suffering or death. And, of course, a corollary, generally associated with the omnipotent God is the conviction that we shouldn't ask these questions. God is in control. God is God. All things happen for a reason. We just need to have faith, and trust that God knows best.

That's not what Frank Tupper spoke to that room of would-be preachers, however. He said, "God always does everything God can do." Everything God *can* do. The comment didn't bother me as much as it obviously bothered some students in the class, but it still rubbed me a bit. I would not be writing this book if it were not still rubbing some, after all these years!

2. Shakespeare, "Hamlet," act 3, scene 1.

But opening my mind to the possibility of a God who truly *cannot* has deepened my spiritual life, enhanced my understanding of the real world, and expanded my view of God. That's right. This God who *can't* is so much bigger, more awe-inspiring, and worthy of worship than the God who always can, though, mostly, does not. The God of my present understanding is more Christlike than the rest of the gods of the world, who wield their power for their own use, at their sole discretion, for their egocentric edification.

My guess is that for many people, robbing God of omnipotent power would, for all practical purposes, essentially destroy God, rub God out of existence. What is a God who *can't*, anyway? Who wants a powerless God? Who needs such a God? Who even conceives of a God who doesn't have "the whole world in his hands"? The power of force is God's most essential nature, power to create infinite worlds, power to control those worlds—and every aspect of my life in this world—that's what God does, isn't it? That's who God *is*, isn't it?

It is common to equate God and ultimate power, almost as synonyms. This as a regrettable fact. Especially in the light of the incarnation of Jesus, a self-giving, dying savior, it is ironic that so many people would allow a love of, or a devotion to power, to destroy God. That is ironic isn't it, because that is what power does: it controls, destroys—even God! Power is destructive and harmful, a tool of egocentric vanity. Love is never any of these things, yet many people simply cannot disassociate "all-powerful" from "God," despite the implications.

Ay . . . there's the rub.

The God We Have Created in Our Image

What would the world be like if the word "God" meant Love for all those for whom the word "God" means omnipotent power? I suspect there are elements of this dichotomy—God as Love versus God as power—in all religions, so it may be appropriate also to ask what the world would be like if Allah or Yahweh or Vishnu were not equated with brute power. I cannot imagine wars fought in the name of love, armies marching into battle beating the drums of self-sacrifice and mutual affection. Can you? I cannot imagine anyone flying a fully loaded commercial jet into a crowded New York skyscraper in the name of a God of sacrificial love. Can you? I cannot imagine anyone abusing his wife and justifying it in the name of grace.

Can you? Such actions flow from systems of domination, which flow from understandings of hierarchy, which are often defined with God at the top, the greatest power.

I fear we have created God in our image, a projection of *our* highest value, a value which is based on our insecurity and our selfishness. I fear we have created God in the image of power—and, having conferred on God the mantel of unqualified omnipotence, the ability to push things around, the ability to do anything, and not to do anything God chooses (in other words, to do nothing if God chooses), power has become God.

But, does this have to be the case? What if we have just misunderstood? Perhaps God really is the greatest "power" in the world, even if we have misunderstood that power. In the fishbowl of God as all power, there is no other way to see God, to understand God, but what if we got outside of the fishbowl?

In other words, limitation is only weakness from the frame of reference of power. If power as the ability to push things around is the highest value, then any limitation to that power would be weakness, because it would, by implication, be inferior to God—the ultimate in pushing things around. But what about love? Love is not weakened by limitations. In fact, some of the greatest examples of love we have are from people regarded by society as weak, yet whose actions—in light of that weakness—display incredible power.

In his bestselling book *The Greatest Generation*, Tom Brokaw details the lives and circumstances of many who endured the ravages of the Great Depression and the Second World War. Despite the challenges they faced, by sacrifice and determination this generation harnessed the vision of freedom and created a path of hope for the future. Their generation has been the most prosperous and defining in the history of our nation. Americans today are products of this generation, many of whom began with almost nothing, in terms of economic or political power. Paradoxically, it was perhaps the absence of any personal power, a power they made available to future generations, that drove many in that day to make such a future for themselves.

The Power that Is Made Perfect in Weakness

Paul's phrase "my power is perfected in weakness" (2 Cor 12:19 NRSV) is worth examining. The word for power, *dunamis*, means "to be able" or "to be capable of," in much the same way the Spanish word for power, *poder*, is translated. "I can go" in Spanish is *puedo ir*, literally "I have the power to go." God's power, in this language from Paul, refers to ability or capacity, not necessarily to raw, coercive force, an all-encompassing strength.

The *Theological Dictionary of the New Testament* contains an extensive discussion of power in the ancient Greek world, tracing the change of understanding of power especially as it relates to the pagan deity and the Jewish and Christian God, and identifies "The Fact of Christ" as decisive in a proper New Testament understanding. "The concept of power is given its decisive impress by the fact of Christ."[3] Power must be understood through the lens of Jesus: his life, death, and resurrection, as displayed in the Gospel witness. The life of Jesus is no example of the capricious use of all power. In view of the cross, quite the opposite is the case. The cross was such a symbol of defeat, humiliation, weakness, that it became perhaps the main hindrance for first century Jews who encountered the Jesus narrative. The apostle Paul made this clear when he said, "We proclaim Christ crucified, a stumbling block to Jews and foolishness to Gentiles" (1 Cor 1:23 NRSV). That symbol of weakness, however, has become the defining Christian symbol of God's power, which is love—and God's love, which is powerful.

The word "perfected" translates the Greek *teleitai*, from the verb which means "to bring to completeness, wholeness." Related to the verb is the noun *telos*, and on his website by the same name, Timothy Breen shares the following insight:

> Loosely translated, *telos* means "purpose" or "outcome." "Endgame" might work too. If you look hard enough, you can see it in the word "telescope"; the implication is that in that instrument, pointed at a distant sailing ship or across a canyon or out toward another galaxy, we can see ("scope out") the *telos*—what's distant, what's at the far end. The telescope offers us new awareness that there is something more beyond.[4]

With these understandings, we might paraphrase Paul's declaration concerning power, perfected in weakness, as this: what God is capable of doing, God's purpose, God only does through love.

---

3. Kittel, *Theological Dictionary*, 2.299.
4. Breen, "Telos," paras. 11–12.

"Noise" and Body Efficiency

In a fascinating *New York Times* article, Natalie Angier writes about the way the human body works, about studies designed to understand how our bodies work, and about how we move. The article praises the work of evolution in developing different components of our bodies. In some cases the body is as efficient as it could be. The eye, for example, has reached what researchers call "optimization." "Photoreceptors operate at the outermost boundary allowed by the laws of physics, which means they are as good as they can be, period."[5] Once you can see individual photons, you can't get any better than that. Some of the body's mechanisms, however, benefit from "noise" or lack of efficiency in their functioning.

Dr. Emanuel Todorov, a neuroscientist at the University of Washington, has extensively studied muscle movement and understands that while we repeat many motions, each individual action is "non-repeatable," that is, we do it slightly differently every time. This may appear sloppy or inefficient, but Dr. Todorov shows that the ability to work with fluctuations, to accept these variations in movement, makes the human body more adaptable and efficient than a robot. For example, "If you're trying to turn on a light switch, who cares if the elbow is down or to the side, or your wrist wobbles?" The brain focuses on the task at hand, and accepts "noise" in the system, using that inefficiency to its highest effect. Trying to operate perfectly, optimizing every movement expends more energy, and, he says, introduces "more noise into the system, amplifying the fluctuations until the entire effort is compromised."[6]

He concludes by saying, "we reach the counterintuitive conclusion that the optimal way to control movement allows a certain amount of fluctuation and noise, a certain *lack of control*"[7] (emphasis added). The body has learned that perfection isn't best. Attempting to overpower each situation is less efficient than working with the imperfections, the inherent weaknesses experienced in any given situation. The body's strength, its innate genius, is its ability to work in and through weakness. "Power is made perfect in weakness" (2 Cor 12:9 NRSV).

Years ago, I got interested in waterskiing as sport, not the kind of "Weekend Wally" recreational activity many people know. I've come to

---

5. Angier, "Seeing the Natural World," para. 2.

6. Angier, "Seeing the Natural World," para. 20.

7. Angier, "Seeing the Natural World," para. 21.

love the no-holds-barred, all-out anaerobic rush that is competitive slalom. Tournament skiing is six aggressive turns through a measured course of buoys, about twenty-five seconds of all-you-can-give-it exertion, a competition matching strength and athletic form against a four-hundred-horse-power inboard engine and the physics of angles and friction.

When I first fell in love with skiing, I was watching an older teenager at the lake send up huge walls of water in each turn. Trying to match that spray, I leaned hard, the ski heading away from the boat, and pulled with all my might. Advancing into the sport, however, I learned that it is not leaning away, tugging against the boat, or the power of *that* angle that creates the perfect spray as much as it is learning to give up that power as you lean back toward the wake.

The middle of the turn is an athletic paradox, the all-out strength of the pull must be matched with a fearless vulnerability of leaning in. Rather than remaining angled against the boat, where the tension of the rope gives stability, you must forego that stability to offer yourself to the turn. Pulling with all your power comes fairly easily, like it's second nature, but learning to lean back toward the boat, learning to accept that feeling of weakness, of losing stability and control, is a much more difficult concept for a skier to learn.

While skiing in a slalom course, the vulnerability of the lean increases with each turn. That lean is the critical moment of weakness that links a pull in one direction to the next pull, made in the opposite direction. Initiating the turn, the ski continues moving outward, away from the boat while the body begins leaning precariously inward. As the ski approaches the buoy, you must trust that lean, dropping your outside hand from the handle, the ski still moving outward as your body follows your hand, and the handle, evermore inward.

At the critical apex of the turn, the coefficient of power literally drops to zero. The ski almost completely stops as you relinquish power for the sake of turning around the buoy and resetting the ski almost 180 degrees. It's useless in a slalom course to be the world's strongest person if you cannot give up that power in the all-important turn.

A common mistake of beginning skiers is to take a defensive posture that limits the amount of lean, the amount of vulnerability given to the turn. Rather than leaning in, offering the handle, and the skier's body toward the boat, the skier's hands stay outside the body, which keeps the body from being exposed to any real lean. This posture is an intuitive reflex, a protection against the weakness which is required in a good slalom turn. It kills any potential for making a good turn. Without accepting the weakness of the lean, the power of the pull itself is useless.

The same basic principle is true in snow skiing, where instructors teach timid students to "ski the fall line." The key to good snow skiing is not defensively angling against the hill, keeping the body safely away from the fall line. Good snow skiers give themselves, fearlessly down the fall line, where the paradox-of-the-turn is equally true: "power is made perfect in weakness" (2 Cor 12:9 NRSV).[8]

On an alpine slope the hands must stay down the hill, which keeps the shoulders perpendicular to the fall line. This position causes the speed to increase, but the worst thing to do at this moment is let your weight fall onto the back of your skis. Balance and form are only achieved by giving yourself to the pull of gravity, leaning down the hill, not fighting it. More athletic skiers sometimes struggle, on water or snow, because they seem wired for powering their way through. As it turns out, the secret to good skiing, as well as to good living, is not the force of power, but learning to acknowledge weakness, to accept vulnerability, to give up power in overcoming adversity.

Healing Magic: An Analogue for God

In chapter 5, I suggested a thought experiment in which my siblings and I were all diagnosed with terminal diseases, and our parents possessed the supernatural power to cure. Would I want my parents to possess that power? The initial, perhaps ill-considered answer is "yes, of course!" We need to think more carefully, however, about what it would mean for parents to possess that power, the power to heal, and to choose which of their children to heal, which not to heal.

In pondering this theoretical situation, an analogue for the way God's power works in the world, it may become obvious that possessing the power to heal, and choosing whom not to heal, would be worse for both children and parents than not possessing such power. The greater power is not a supernatural or magical healing ability, but the more difficult discipline of presence and grace. I would rather have my parents' ever-present love than

8. I've often thought of the good theology embedded in that instruction, and when I hear "ski the fall line," I can't help but think of Adam and Eve, that so-called "fall of humanity" theologians have spoken of for generations.

to know they possessed the power to heal me but elected only to heal one of my siblings, or vice versa.

Why would the love and power of God be any different than that? Why would it seem more godly to ascribe to the Divine the brute force to control disease and disaster rather than to affirm an innate love, at all cost, accepting the weaknesses and limitations of that love no matter the outcome of personal or natural tragedies? I can only imagine that such a theology of power is born of a very human preference for control over presence, for strength over service, for power over love—none of which we see in the life and story of Jesus of Nazareth.

Looking for an Answer: Proof Texting and the Bible

Many will ask about the Bible: "But, doesn't the Bible say . . .?" It is clear that if we only look to the Bible to proof text our answers, Scripture can be found, used and abused, to justify almost any bias. So, yes, proof texts justifying a God of power and manipulative control abound. After his encounter with God, the suffering Job returns to God: "I know that you can do all things, and that no purpose of yours can be thwarted" (Job 42:1–2 NRSV).

On the other hand, let us admit that it might be difficult to find Scripture explicitly naming the limitation of God's power that I am proposing. I have been quoting Paul's words to the church at Corinth: "God's power is made perfect in *weakness*" (2 Cor 12:9 NRSV; emphasis added), though naysayers will object that such weakness is our weakness, not God's. That objection might be the same for Mark 6:5–6, a story in which Jesus "could do no deed of power there" since any lack of power was a result of the people's lack of faith, not Jesus's impotence.

The only unequivocal "cannot" I can find in a literal text is in 2 Tim 2:13: "If we are faithless, God remains faithful for God *cannot* deny God's own self" (emphasis added). God cannot be unfaithful. God cannot fail the test of love, though any good biblical literalists would easily dismiss this "cannot" as not pertaining to omnipotent power but to God's integrity. I want to be honest about the Bible, acknowledging that it is difficult to find a simple proof text of a God of limited power. But let's also acknowledge that proof texting is only a satisfactory game for the proof texter.

Scriptural interpretation has been a stumbling block for as long as there have been sacred scriptures. As careful theologians and students of the Bible understand, there is no such thing as an intelligent literal reading of the Bible. The honest, simple truth is that no one reads free from the influence of his/her own biases.[9] Time, place, gender, age, education, and experience, these and many more factors influence our reading of any text.

Noting that scriptural interpretation has always been difficult is not a radical hypothesis, just an honest observation. The Bible was understood very differently in a pre-Copernican world, because acknowledging that the earth travels around the sun, not vice versa, makes quite a difference to your worldview. Precolonial and postcolonial understandings of God and humanity, as well as ecclesiology and eschatology, differ greatly. Equally earth-shaking advancements like emancipation, women's suffrage, LGBTQ rights, etc. continue to enhance our readings of the Bible. Our readings are always conditioned by our experience. Even if one claims the Bible is literally or objectively true, it must be read, filtered, understood through our not-so-literal and always-subjective experience.

The historical/critical method of biblical inquiry, which began in the great universities of Europe in the early nineteenth century, insisted on studying the Bible as any other book. If the Bible was inspired, it should and would stand against any critique, even if judged by the same academic methods that were applied to any other subject. So, the Bible should be judged historically, linguistically, scientifically, culturally, contextually, and should not be protected as a qualitatively different kind of book. That method has guided academic study of the Bible, and it has deepened the understandings and faith of critically aware Christians ever since. The least of what a critical reading of Scripture does, however, is to force us to acknowledge that *interpretation* is never optional.

If abusing the Bible, making it justify slavery for nearly two thousand years, is the only case in point, none other is needed. Inevitably, we go to the Scriptures with our own biases, either looking for literal words to support our views or twisting the interpretation of texts into the support of our preconceived notions. The Christian conviction is that the only way out of this morass is not the literal Bible (that understanding led us into the morass to begin with), but the Living Word: Jesus himself.

If Jesus is the lens through which we view God, and the death of Jesus is the lens through which we view his life, the prism of *limitation* shines a clear light on the work of God. In the life of Jesus, it is clear that God works

9. Every text, no matter how simple, must be interpreted by the reader. Does "thou shalt not kill" (Exod 20:13 NRSV) negate self-defense? Just war? Capital punishment? The text says, "Thou shalt *not kill*." Period. Any understanding requires interpretation.

not through the force of omnipotence but through the life-changing work of love. Whenever, wherever, however . . . love finds a way. With Jesus's example, we need no other.

Can we imagine the Christian narrative if Jesus *had* called ten thousand angels, had fought back the Romans with the sword, had pummeled them into submission to become the military and political savior that many, even his disciples, hoped he would become? And what kind of savior would that have made him? What kind of kingdom would he have ruled?

I ask if we can imagine that, but, clearly, we *can* imagine that theology. It is all around us—promoted in the secular philosophies of every nation and taught in the pious dogmas which have perverted the pure origins of every religion. Those ways, however, whether secular or religious, do not reflect the theology of the cross, which accepts the limitations of love, the brokenness and suffering of a fallen world. The theology of the cross accepts those limitations—because there is no other way, because there is no other choice. In Jesus we see a God who is determined to work in this world—a world filled with limitations—and not just above it.

The cross inverts the failed power of force to show the power of weakness. It is the way of love, a "more excellent way" (1 Cor 12:31 NRSV), but if it is only pretending, only feigning powerlessness for dramatic effect, only withholding power as a facade to draw in the unsuspecting, or only delaying power to justify the use of even greater power, then it is not love, but an abusive, intrusive force in disguise.

Playing Games: "Godness" and a Theology of Reality

As I have noted, some maintain in their theology a caveat that God *had* all power—but relinquished that power at creation. They say God still has all power—but practices a kind of self-restraint. They believe God self-limits omnipotent power for the sake of natural laws, the consistency and order they bring. In this view, God *could* do anything, but if God ever did choose to intervene, stepping in to tinker with nature's laws, then the universe would cease to exist as we know it. (I can hear Michael Stipe singing, even now: "It's the end of the world as we know it . . . and I feel fine!")[10]

This logic may even pass a strange scientific muster—because if there *were* a supernatural force that intervened into and contradicted Newton's natural laws, that intervention *would* change physics and biology and

10. R.E.M., "It's the End."

chemistry, *would* alter the world as we know it, forever. Think of it: if Joshua's legendary tale were understood as historical fact, if the sun did truly stand still in the sky, then what could be relied upon after that? The biology of the planet is dependent upon the sun's consistent journey. Gravity is a factor of the tug from our celestial neighbor. The world's chemistry originated in the sun's internal, infernal conversion of helium. And meteorologists, well, how would they ever again give us accurate forecasts? And what about sleep? Who would ever know when to go to sleep, ever again?

So, play that game if you must. Demand that logic if you will, in order to justify a "Godness" premised on brute force—but this idea, that God rejected all-power or self-limits omnipotent power, that kind of theology requires one to say that the only possible God that can be reconciled to this world is a deity who *could* stop all evil but literally chooses not to stop evil. I simply cannot live with that kind of God. Perhaps more importantly, *I am not willing to say there is no other way to define or conceive of the reality of God.*

What is more, following the logic of the self-limited-omnipotent God, the practical outcome brings us precisely to the theology I am proposing. In other words, if God has literally limited God's power—so what we see and experience is an omnipotent God with limited power—then what we've actually got, in the real world in which we live, is a God who can't!

I am just asking, why the need for such theological gymnastics? Why not practice a theology of reality, a view that is simpler from the outset, and which comports better with the realities of science and the evidence of our experience? That theology of reality says in the experience of this very real world, God is real, and God is present in dynamic ways, present with us and in us—but God exists and is made manifest only as Love, a Love which is the only good power the world will ever know.

I just want to give up the games. Our theology needs to more closely align with the reality of our lived experience. Why should we have to work so hard to overcome the contradictions of the all-powerful-but-loving God in a world with so much suffering? The truth is that those contradictions are only inherent with a particular literal reading of the Bible and within a theology that defends omnipotence at all costs.

If God did not create the world this way, or if the world is not God's to manipulate in every detail, then God is not responsible for the suffering. God is only the light that shines in such darkness. So, why play the games to make God conform to the ideas that societies have so long attributed to the Divine, ideas that are predicated on fear and superstition?

If God is Love, we have nothing to fear.

If God is Love, no superstitious rituals are needed to appease God's wrath.

If God is Love, we need only to grow up in faith and let God be the God Jesus taught us to see.

God always does everything Love can do. And when God can't, God loves, still.

It is not my purpose in this book to try to take away anything—no one's theology, no one's faith, no one's God. My emphasis is not the rejection of a wrong way of thinking, but the invitation to an exciting new way of understanding. I view my journey as additive to my faith rather than subtractive.

Some years ago, I met a woman who had spent two exciting but challenging years in seminary. To be fair to that seminary, she did not complete the educational curriculum, but that incomplete education had failed her. In her studies she had been introduced to the discipline of "demythologizing" the Bible; that is, viewing the miraculous elements of biblical accounts through purely scientific or historical lenses, thus rejecting them as historical, factual accounts. In place of a mythology filled with literal miracles, demythologizing proposes more spiritual understandings as if to say, "So what that Jesus did not literally walk on the water? He changed my heart, my life, my world!"

The two-year seminarian, however, reflected that she had been out of the church and away from organized religion mostly ever since, because, as she sadly said, "I got 'demythologized' but never 'remythologized' again." What a tragedy when new ideas only strip from us our old theologies, like throwing out the baby with the bathwater.

That is not what I am proposing.

"The God Who Can't" in no way denies or rejects God! I have never rejected either the idea or the experience of God, and I am not suggesting a denunciation of divinity. Quite to the contrary, "The God Who Can't" is the powerful God of presence and love. "The God Who Can't" is an idea that can allow us to believe, without walking in conflict with everything our twenty-first century world experiences as real. "The God Who Can't" is a reality that gives meaning and purpose, direction and aim to our lives.

"The God Who Can't" is still God!

And "The God Who Can't" still *does*—because love is always action.

The world will fail us. Family and friends will fail us, too. It's just the way it works. By happenstance or malice, bad things happen, even to good people. God neither intentionally plans nor specifically allows tragedy and heartache. When John Fox was the coach of the NFL's Carolina Panthers, he became known for stating the obvious: "It is what it is."[11] He's right. Life just happens. It is what it is. We need to quit blaming God for the pills and the ills and learn to find God in the aftermath of life's storms.[12] When it's all over, when the shattered pieces of life and faith are lying at our feet, God will be there. God will be there, coming behind us to gather up all that is left, because God has been there, broken with us, for us. Knowing the suffering and pain that comes only to those who love, God heals. Not with power but with love.

"My power is made perfect in weakness" (2 Cor 12:9 NRSV).

God. Always. Does. Everything. Love. **CAN.** Do.

11. Reporting for the *Greensboro News and Record*, Tim Whitmire records it this way: "A 37-17 thumping by the Tennessee Titans on Sunday is neither the beginning of the end nor a blessing in disguise for the Carolina Panthers, coach John Fox said this week. 'It's one loss, and it is what it is,' Fox said, using one of his trademark phrases to put the defeat in perspective." Whitmire, "Coach," para. 1–2.

12. See the appendix at the end of the book, "A Prayer for Maryanne," which I wrote in the aftermath of the devastating loss of a young mother and wife, her family and friends trying to make sense of the tragedy and to find God in the pain.

8

God. Always. Does. Everything. Love. Can. **Do.** (God before Us)

"Behold, I am doing a new thing." (Isa 43:19 NRSV)

When I talk about God, I'm not talking about a divine being who is behind, trying to drag us back to a primitive, barbaric, regressive, prescientific age when we believed earth was flat and the center of the universe. I believe that God isn't backward-focused—opposed to reason, liberation, and progress—but instead is pulling us and calling us and drawing all of humanity forward—as God always has—into greater and greater peace, love, justice, connection, honesty, compassion, and joy. I want you to see how the God we see at work in the Bible is actually ahead of people, tribes, and cultures as God always has been. Far too many people in our world have come to see God as back there, primitive, not-that-intelligent, dragging everything backward to where it used to be. I don't understand God to be stuck back there, and I want you to experience this pull forward as a vital, active reality in your day-to-day life as you see just what God has been up to all along with every single one of us.

ROB BELL[1]

1. Bell, *What We Talk about,* 19.

Questions to Prompt Your Reading

What "good old days" from the past do you idealize? What was so good about them? What was not so good about those days?

What truths have changed from your childhood to now?

Has your idea of God changed? Has the idea of God changed in our culture?

Do you believe in free will? What does this mean? How free is "free"?

Does God know the future? Can you really be free if God knows everything you are going to choose, everywhere you're going to go, everything you're going to do?

How does God change the future?

What is the relationship of God's power to your freedom? Of God's love to that freedom?

Going Back to the Good Old Days . . . Where? Why?

The Bible opens onto the garden of Eden, that pristine paradise of no tears and crying, no toil and dying, which sounds pretty good, but think of what was missing in that presumed utopia. Eve never enjoyed the refreshing, cleansing feeling of a nice, hot shower, or the splendid feeling of newly cleaned sheets on the bed, since nothing ever got dirty in Eden. Adam never knew the joy of an ice-cold lemonade to quench his thirst, and he never came in famishing, and felt the satisfaction of a good, home-cooked meal settling into an empty, grateful stomach. You know, "hunger," what did that mean? There were no championship game victories to celebrate, and there were no losers to know the consolation of a mother's careful touch. And, you know how good just a little bit of poison ivy feels, just enough that you can enjoy the relentless relief of a little scratching? Oh, that feeling is sooooo good. So, how could it possibly have been paradise without just a little bit of poison ivy!? No aches to soothe, no hungers to satisfy, no challenges to overcome, no itches to scratch . . .

And we want to go back there? Why!?

The memory of that perfection, however, seems like it is imprinted ever so faintly onto our evolved and inherited DNA, because it is tantalizingly strong. Going back, getting back to some good old days when everything was just like it should have been, that idea has been a perennial focus of poisonous politics and repressive religion since, well, since the good old days! I don't know why people cannot remember that the good old days never were. Every age has its golden charms, but there is no Camelot. Everything wasn't so good back then, and a lot of what appears to have glittered wasn't gold, either.

Yet, going back, looking back, wishing for what (never) was, however misunderstood that idea, seems irresistible to the human creature. Those two "in the beginning" narratives in Genesis (Gen 1 and 2), imbued with the idea of a pristine perfection, have been a curse we may never cure. Maybe the idea of going back is, itself, a kind of original sin—the sin of fundamental longing, our most selfish desire, the desire to be freed from responsibility. Adam and Eve are pictured much like children: everything has been given to them, done for them. All they have to do is enjoy. They have no troubles and no toil, no deadlines, and no duties. Who could not love that?

But what is there to love about such a childish neglect of our potential?

No, going back is not our future. Not only is returning to any past a physical impossibility, the idea that we have lost something they had, something that was better, is demoralizing and short sighted. Can you imagine any of our ancestors, of any prior age, not wanting to change positions with *us*? Would you really want to change positions with any of them? Think of our creature comforts, our vast and diverse areas of knowledge, even our treatment of one another. The 24/7 media culture brings natural disasters and acts of violence into our homes on an hourly basis, but the violence is less than at any point in our human history. Try to imagine coping with earthquake or famine or disease without all the modern means at our disposal. The Christian Church, in particular, seems infatuated with the golden years of the 1950s, a kind of *Leave It to Beaver* world where everyone stayed married and everyone went to church. I invite you to examine that assumption, and, if you are old enough, remember back to all that wasn't so glittering about that black-and-white era. (It was, literally, a black and white era.)

I bring all of this up because this book, to this point, has also been a retrospective, a looking back at ideas of God. As we contemplate this last word, "do," however, we need to look forward. We need to "lay aside every weight . . . and run with perseverance the race that is set *before* us" (Heb 12:1 NRSV; emphasis added). God is not back there. God never has been.

We will always miss what is most-essentially divine if we are looking for God in the past. The past is dead, gone, only a memory, and if God is anything at all, God is life, possibility, hope, future. When we look back, particularly looking back on the experiences of faith as testified in Scripture, we need to remember that God was always in front of the people. From our present vantage, that is all behind us, but during those experiences, as the people lived them, God was in front of the people, always challenging them to new thoughts, better ideas, bigger challenges, a brighter future.

We are looking back, but we are looking back on these people who were looking forward, always finding a new God being revealed. John Mogabgab, once editor of *Weavings Journal*, introduced one volume with the reminder that "God continually revises and expands who we think God is supposed to be. 'For my thoughts are not your thoughts, neither are your ways my ways, says the Lord' (Isa. 55:8, RSV)."[2] New thoughts, better ideas—even of God—should always be before us.

2. Mogabgab, "Trust," 2–3.

Looking Back on the Future

It is no mistake that the dimensions of the front windshield of a car and the rearview mirror are not reversed. While it is helpful to see where you have been, it is quite dangerous to focus only on the rearview mirror when you drive. With this perspective in mind, there is an irony in looking back on those stories of faith—because the God of those narratives always represents a confident future. Moving forward with God never guarantees a future free from uncertainties. The future is always uncertain. It will be unfortunate, then, if we try to freeze any of those moments in time, any of the issues of that day, with their proclamations about faith or revelations of God, and claim to find in a retrospective view the affirmation of static, unchanging dogmas. Jesus reminded his disciples, "When the Spirit of truth comes, he will guide you into all the truth" (John 16:13 NRSV). This promise is for all times. The Spirit is still guiding us into truth. Truth will always be ahead of us.

God is truth, the unchanging truth of justice and mercy, grace and goodness, forgiveness and peace, the truth of faith, hope, and love—but the understanding and experience and application even of transcendent truth does change over time. Let us not be confused about this. Truth doesn't change, but our scenery certainly does.

Changing Perspectives and Progress

Travelling through the mountains can shed light on this sometimes-disorienting affirmation. When you travel up a mountain, the location of the destination never changes, but as the road winds, the peak may be visible at one moment out the right-side window and a few minutes later out the left. If the road winds enough, as mountains (and life) are prone to do, on one of those hairpin turns the pinnacle may even appear in the rearview mirror for a time. The endpoint has not changed—nor does truth—but if we are moving forward, we cannot know what is coming, what turns or unexpected detours we may encounter, and that journey makes the landscape appear quite varied. At times the winding road may obscure the destination altogether. Faith means pressing on, trusting God to guide our way. Ironically, it is *progress* that makes the destination *appear* to change. It is only the person who never sets out on the journey who always sees the top of the mountain in the same place.

Jesus made this truth clear when he said, "You have heard that it was said" (I can see the top of the mountain over there), "but I say to you" (wait, how did it get over *there*?). Killing someone and just being angry with them (Matt 5:21–22 NRSV) seem like two completely different truths. Having an extramarital affair and just looking at someone with lusty eyes (Matt 5:27–28 NRSV) may seem to be completely different views of justice, but Jesus was trying to broaden our understanding, encouraging us to take the next step up the mountain, risking the sometimes-distorting view that comes in all those turns. Taking that journey, however, is the only way to get to the top.

"You have heard that it was said, 'An eye for an eye, and a tooth for a tooth'" (Matt 5:38 NRSV). Though this principle of measured retribution is far from the kind of justice Jesus envisioned, it was a step in that direction when Moses issued the command to an ancient people. Prior to a system of equal retaliation, chaos ruled. If someone stole one sheep from neighbor, retaliation might have resulted in the victim taking the perpetrator's whole flock of sheep in return. The loss of an entire flock was a disproportionate cost compared to the loss of one animal. If one member of a tribe was killed in battle, retribution might have resulted in killing the enemy's whole clan, razing their village, taking all their possessions. In that environment of un-bridled revenge an "eye for an eye" was visionary, revolutionary.

Looking back, we can see that the people were moving "up the moun-tain" even though "an eye for an eye" appears to lead in a completely differ-ent direction than Jesus's instruction to "turn the other cheek" (Matt 5:39 NRSV). Jesus was changing the people's direction, but not their ultimate destination. The destination is the same as the revolutionary truth Moses taught.

One day, preachers said slavery is ordained of God, because the Bible says so. (If you read the Bible in that certain way, it still does.) Almost over-night, however, most preachers came to understand slavery as an unthink-able violation of the human-to-human and human-to-divine relationship that God intends. Since we now affirm the equality of all people regardless the color of their skin, at least in theory, what was once blasphemy has become truth.

One day, women cannot vote or work outside the home, and they certainly can't preach, because the Bible says so. Again, if you are condi-tioned to read so narrowly, you can still find the Bible saying so—but when we recognize that our cultural and intellectual landscape has significantly changed, another "blasphemy" becomes truth.

Too many people still read a handful of culturally conditioned texts as a means of condemning members of the LGBTQIA+ community, but medical, psychological, and social research have helped us to turn the tide on that once-blasphemy as well, recognizing the truth that God has made all, and loves all. As the Irish playwright and political activist George Bernard Shaw rightly noted, "All great truths begin as blasphemies."[3]

The judgment that homosexuality is an abomination and the affirmation of the homosexual person as made in God's image, just as normal and as natural as her or his heterosexual counterpart—these two positions may seem to represent two contradictory truths. If we understand our history, however, and understand that our view at any given point in history depends on where we are in the journey "up the mountain," we will know that the destination has not changed. Truth remains. For our relationship with African Americans and women and homosexuals, the destination has always been equality and acceptance and recognition. Those goals have not changed. God has not changed. Truth has not changed. But our vision has changed. Thanks be to God.

Truth: Destination or Guide?

More of our vision needs to change, and it will, because the Spirit keeps moving us forward "into all truth." It is worth pondering this metaphor, however. I have suggested the metaphor of a journey whose destination is truth, but an alternate metaphor could envision truth as our guide along the "long and winding road."[4] In this second metaphor, truth is not the destination, truth is a guide to the destination, which is always unknown. If truth becomes the destination, it may be dangerously easy to harden our view of truth at any given moment, making truth into an idol which, ironically, keeps us from seeing God. Maybe this is the more appropriate metaphor, then: truth, as we can see it and understand it at any present moment, as a guide. Understood in this way, truth leads us into more truth, which just keeps leading us.

Some may ask, "So, where *are* we going? Where is all of this leading us? What really is our destination?" These questions, however, may be

3. "Books," para. 3.
4. The Beatles, "Long and Winding Road."

antithetical to true faith. The journey of faith, as God told old Abram, will always be "to a land I will show you" (Gen 12:1 NRSV). I wonder if the father of our faith would have signed up for the journey if God had told him how long that journey was going to be, and how difficult. If he had known he might never reach a destination, that the whole point of faith is the journey itself, even when it feels like wandering in the wilderness, would he have signed up?

We do not know where God is leading us. That's the whole point—it could not be called faith otherwise. We *can* be assured, however, that it will be forward. We do not disparage our past by saying that we never want to go back there. On the contrary, we honor our past by recognizing that only because of the journey our forebears traveled have we arrived at our present. We learn who we are by looking at our past. We can see where God has been, giving us assurance that God will be with us on the journey. But when we look back, we are seeing where God *was*, not where God is. Furthermore, we should hope that our descendants will outtravel us, that the landscape and the truths they see will be different, brighter, truer, still, as God continues to go before us, leading us "into all truth."

The thirteenth century Italian intellectual, Thomas Aquinas, is one of the most influential minds in the history of Christian thought. He understood much when he said that we can know *that* God is, and what God is *not*, but we can never know what God *is*. Could it be that our insatiable desire to look back is a desperate attempt, idolatrous at its heart, to know what God is? Is our looking back an attempt to use the experiences of others in a kind of childish attempt to clearly and cleanly define the Divine? Can anyone else's experience of God stand for mine?

An idol is anything that is created to supplant God. There are no adequate pictures of God or definitions of God, and claiming any of these as absolute, these pictures of God from our past, is to make a kind of "graven image" in the place of God (Exod 20:4 NRSV). Maybe those powerful images of God, formed by our ancestors in the crucible of their own experiences with God, can only be idols for us. They are images created by someone else's experience. The record of that experience can only point us to *their* image of God. That image, however, is not God, and that image is behind us. It will almost certainly not be what we see in our own experience of God.

Honoring the Past without Looking Back

The strange but vivid story of the destruction of Sodom and Gomorrah is sadly misunderstood and often used maliciously as justification to condemn homosexuals, perhaps even to "rain sulphur and fire" (Gen 19:24 NRSV) on them, as was the fate of these cities. The sin of Sodom and Gomorrah, however, was specifically not homosexuality, this according to the Bible itself.[5] The text in Genesis does not indicate the nature of Sodom's offense, only that the people "were wicked, great sinners" (Gen 13:13 NRSV). God decides to destroy the city for its wickedness, but sends two angels to warn the main character, Lot, of the impending fate. They tell Lot to take his wife and daughters and to flee, and they warn, "Do not look back" (Gen 19:17 NRSV).

Like too many of us, though, Lot's wife could not resist. There was something about her home, wicked as it was, wrong as it had been, even destined for doom, that still captivated her. Even as fire was raining on the city, which should have been a clear indication there was no future there, she could not let it go, and she turned to look back. For doing so she will forever be remembered as the nameless woman, only "Lot's wife," who "became a pillar of salt" (Gen 19:26 NRSV).

The past holds that same attraction for us, doesn't it? No matter what wrongs it represents there seems a yearning to turn, to return. Maybe the truth for us today, coming from this odd, ancient tale of destruction is that even if we want to go back, our past is not there, and it never will be. Time has destroyed it. We must move on. God is not to be found in looking back, maintaining old truths, old superstitions, old understandings, old traditions.

A song from my religious childhood, a popular church chorus for fellowship gatherings, said, "Give me that old time religion . . . it's good enough for me."[6] It seems that kind of religion is good enough for a lot of folks these days, as it always has been, people who want to look back, clinging fearfully to a past that is already history. (Is there any other kind of past?) The new becomes old, always, because time moves on.

5. "This was the guilt of your sister Sodom: she and her daughters had pride, excess of food, and prosperous ease, but did not aid the poor and needy" (Ezek 16:49 NRSV).
6. "Old Time Religion."

The Pace of Change

The future brings understandable anxiety, but clinging to the past will not slow the pace of time and the inevitable change that comes with it. There is a great deal of anxiety in our culture today. The pace of change is amazing and terrifying. A "knowledge doubling curve," designed by the futurist Buckminster Fuller, estimates that before 1900 human knowledge doubled every century. It now doubles in thirteen months, and one prediction suggests computer advancement and internet connectivity will soon reduce that time to twelve hours.[7] The human brain cannot keep that pace, and the overwhelming magnitude of change comes as an assault on our psyche.

The Pew Research Center has been tracking the religious practice of Americans for decades and several years ago began noting the rise of Americans who claim no religious affiliation. This group, while still a minority, now represents the fastest growing religious demographic in their studies. "The religiously unaffiliated (also called the 'nones') now account for 23% of the adult population, up from 16% in 2007."[8] White Americans, who have enjoyed majority status since the founding of this country, are estimated to lose that majority by the year 2045, according to a 2018 report by the Brookings Institute.

> The shift is the result of two trends. First, between 2018 and 2060, gains will continue in the combined racial minority populations, growing by 74 percent. Second, during this time frame, the aging white population will . . . experience a long-term decline through 2060, a consequence of more deaths than births.[9]

In 2015 the Public Religion Research Institute reported that for the first time, the US is no longer a majority white Protestant nation.[10]

In a short amount of time a great deal of change has occurred in this country. In the face of that change many are clinging to a comfortable past. The hopeful possibilities for the future are overlooked in a wash of fear that the unknown always brings. Cultural and technological and medical and religious changes all signify a rapidly changing world. The future is uncertain. There is much about which to be anxious.

7. Schilling, "Knowledge Doubling Every 12 Months," para. 1.

8. "U.S. Public Becoming Less Religious," para. 5.

9. Frey, "US Will Become 'Minority White,'" para. 2.

10. Blosser, "For First Time," para. 2.

Our anxiety, however, will neither slow the pace of time nor reverse these changes. And change will continue. We must embrace the change, and the future, for, as the prophet Isaiah said, in the words of God: "Behold, I am doing a new thing" (Isa 43:19 NRSV)—and that was almost three thousand years ago!

Where is God in this changing world? God will always be found in newness, in new understanding and new revelation. We need not fear any tomorrow. God goes before us. Writing about Teilhard de Chardin's revolutionary theology, Georgetown University professor John Haught addresses our evolutionary past and our theological future. "Evolution," he says, "rules out the possibility that paradise ever existed."[11] The pinnacle of human history is not the idealized past of the fabled garden of Eden. This scientific fact is one that must be embraced by the church. That loss, however, should not be a cause for despair, for Teilhard's theology was future-looking and optimistic. The pinnacle of human history is still before us. The idealized *future* awaits!

It is the job of good theology, especially in light of the settled science of an evolving universe, to help the church reframe its vision, from longing for a past that never was, to working for a brighter future that can be. Haught says,

> What must be our new thoughts about God in the context of an unfinished universe? The question needs to be asked . . . to facilitate the [Christian] tradition's survival and thriving far into the future . . . the intellectual respectability of theology demands our bringing together in new ways current scientific understanding of the universe and Christianity's persistent hope for new creation.[12]

Let the church hear God saying, today and always, "Behold, I am [still] doing a new thing."

God and Our Future

With all this talk of past and future, of God "before us," let me make clear my understanding of God's role in this future. Just as I reject the idea that God has controlled the past, I do not believe God controls, sees, or knows the future.

11. Haught, "Teilhard de Chardin," 7.
12. Haught, "Teilhard de Chardin," 11.

One of the earliest theological conversations I remember engaging was with a high school coach who had shared with me his belief in predestination.[13] My coach said that God knows the future, even knows the moment we will all die, so the future is not open. God controls the future. Being a good Baptist, believing in free will, I objected. "Yes, God knows the future," I said, "God can see the future, knows what you're going to choose, but that doesn't take away our free will. You have free choice. It doesn't have to make sense to us. God is God!"

I did not win that argument, and I should not have. My logic was wrong. I still believe our lives and our deaths are not determined in advance, so I believe my coach was wrong on that point, but my argument made no logical sense. There is no logical way for God (even the God in whom I *then* believed) to know or see tomorrow, and for that knowledge not to determine the outcomes of tomorrow. If God knows, for example, that I am going to fall and break my leg tomorrow, is there any possible thing that could be done to avoid that fate? The answer is no. For God to *know*, would be for God to *determine* that outcome.

The God in whom I now believe, this God who can't, does not know or see the future, not specifically. The future is open. We are truly free, and that freedom is God's greatest gift to us. To impinge on freedom at any point, in this life or the next, would negate the very definition of freedom. Loving our children means raising them to be self-sufficient, learning to trust them, celebrating when we send them off to be on their own. As difficult as that is, setting them free is the greatest display of our confidence and love. Denying freedom would strip the word love of its full meaning.

I have been arguing in this book that God does not control all things because God *cannot* control all things. What God *can* do God always does. Here, I want to add that even if God *could* control all things, for the sake of freedom, freedom that is essential to love, God would not.

As a parent, if I could save my child from running in the street and being hit by a car, I would certainly do so—as would God. God always does everything Love can do. On the other hand, if I could control my child's every move, determine her destiny, even if that meant guaranteeing the future, eliminating all possible street collisions, even potentially fatal consequences, I hope I am wise enough that I would choose not to exercise

---

13. I have since learned to recognize an error in his language/argument. What my coach was affirming was predeterminism, which is quite different from John Calvin's doctrine of predestination, but an exposition of Calvin's doctrine is not my interest here.

that option. What would it mean for my child to have no ultimate freedom? Would he ever really grow up? What would a knowledge of this determinism do for his self-identity, his self-esteem? Could he ever really have any faith? Could he ever truly love?

It is the affirmation of faith that God is ever before us, preparing a way, but this affirmation need not mean God knows, and, therefore, determines our way for us. The future is open. We are free. Love is our proof.

Another image that stays with me was also shared by Frank Tupper. The image provides a metaphor that attempts to reconcile the paradox of God going before us yet allowing full human freedom. The picture is of God as a weaver, bringing together all the threads of our lives, creating the tapestry that is our past, present, and future. As the weaver, God is before us, gathering up the loose threads, putting them all together, yet the weaver is standing with her back to the future. As such, she is as blind to tomorrow as we are. The future is open, not predetermined, yet without the weaver, there would be no tapestry, we would have no future.

All that is new and good, every tomorrow, is a gift from the God who loves too much to destroy our essential freedom. We have limited our understanding of God by a narrow vision of power, and because that is all we can see, we have not begun to glimpse the bigness of God. The conviction of faith claims that one day we will see: "For now we see in a mirror, dimly, but then we will see face to face" (1 Cor 13:12 NRSV). With eyes of faith, opened by love, we will see the God who goes before us as the source of all good possibility.

"Behold, I am doing a new thing" (Isa 43:19 NRSV).

God. Always. Does. Everything. Love. Can. **Do.**

AN ASIDE: POWER

An online science textbook asserts: $Power = \dfrac{Work}{Time}$

> Power is a measure of the amount of work that can be done in a
> given amount of time. . . . Power can be calculated from work and
> time using the equation.[1]

For many people, God's essence, God's nature is virtually equivalent to
power, the ability in the temporal world to do actual, physical work. God is
raw power, ultimate power. The so called omni-attributes of God are quoted
often: God is omniscient (all knowing), omnipresent (present everywhere
at all times), and omnipotent (all-powerful). In this understanding, to deny
that God could do anything, anywhere, at any time is to deny God. The
theological formula is simpler than the above, and almost as mathematical
in its certainty: God = power.

In this regard God is defined in and by the physical world. If God can't
push things around (moving the tornado), direct biological processes (pre-
venting the disease), control the outcomes (curing the cancer), then who *is*
God, *what* is God? What good is God? God is a force of nature. God works
in the world, pushing things around. The trick of faith is to make sure we're
on the benevolent end of the pushing.

The aspect of omnipotence that is often overlooked is that if God is
the power of the universe, working for you, closing the business deal, giving
you the winning touchdown, blessing you with a healthy child, God must
also be responsible for all the bad things. Faith becomes a kind of divine/
human game: How can I live well enough, pray hard enough, practice faith
enough to ensure the power always falls in my favor?

---

1. CK-12, "13.3 Power."

If power is the game, we will always be beholden, begging, cowering a bit before all the possibility. But what if God is more than that? More even than omnipotence?

What if God's power is not the ability to push things around, to pick and choose whom to bless and when, to control the outcome of every game? What if God's power is even more powerful than that?

Life's experience leads many people to know that control is overrated. For the things that really matter, power itself is limited. You can push things around in your favor only so long, and, even then, doing so is not a means to fulfilment and happiness. In the end, it's not power, but love that really changes the things that matter.

Once you realize the limitation of power, and can see the power of love, you can begin to wrap your mind around a God whose presence, without power-as-force, may be the most powerful thing you ever conceived. Do not sentimentalize this. It's not warm fuzzy love, puppy love, Cupid and happily-ever-after love. "God is love" (1 John 4:8 NRSV) does not mean all of life is a peach. It's not that at all. The crass adage "life sucks, and then you die" is still true. If the real formula is "God = Love," all the horrible things that *can* happen still *might* happen.

The difference is that once we can give up the formula "God = power" then we can begin to grow up in our own strength, while becoming alert to a different kind of power. People who have been there, in the grip of the worst that can happen, yet who have experienced presence, real love in those moments, those people will tell you that presence (Maybe we should write *Presence*.) is a different kind of power. Having experience that kind of Presence, they would never exchange it for a distant deity who sometimes chooses to push things around in their favor.

9

Conclusion:
God Always Does Everything Love Can Do.
(God in Us)

"For the [kin-dom] of God is within you." (Luke 17:21)[1]

She say, "Celie, tell the truth, have you ever found God in church? I never did.
I just found a bunch of folks hoping for [God] to show. Any God I ever felt in
church I brought with me. And I think all the other folks did too. They come to
church to *share* God, not find God."

ALICE WALKER[2]

1. I have referred to the "kingdom of God" elsewhere in this book, though it seems
appropriate from here to the end to utilize this variation, as explained by Diana Butler
Bass: "The noted theologian Ada María Isasi-Díaz recalls originally hearing 'kin-dom'
. . . as an alternative to the language of 'kingdom,' a word fraught with colonial oppression and imperial violence. 'Jesus,' she wrote, 'used "kingdom of God" to evoke . . . an
alternative "order of things"' over and against the political context of the Roman Empire
and its Caesar, the actual kingdom and king at the time. . . Christians have often failed
to recognize that 'kingdom' was an inadequate and incomplete way of speaking of God's
governance, not a call to set up their own empire. Isasi-Díaz argues that 'kin-dom,' an
image of *la familia*, the liberating family of God working together for love and justice, is
a metaphor closer to what Jesus intended." Bass, "Kin-dom of God," para. 1–2.

2. Walker, *Color Purple*, 193.

Questions to Prompt Your Reading

In the way you conceive of God, where is God? In heaven? On a throne? In nature? In your heart? What does this location tell you about what God means for you?

A friend of mine said, "God does not exist outside human consciousness." What does this mean to you?

What does the word supernatural mean to you—separate or completely different from the natural world, or is it the superlative of nature itself? Is God *supernatural*?

In this book I have been trying to make the case for a God who is very real, but very different from the "God" many people understand. If God only existed in human consciousness or within you, if God was not supernatural (as in, separate from nature) . . . could that still be God for you?

How have you experienced God? Could you make a persuasive case that that experience was not just physiological, an emotional response to the grandeur or nature or the beauty of a symphony or the power of human intimacy or just the exuberance of life? Do we need to be able to make that case? To whom?

Tell 'Em

The old preaching adage defines a good sermon outline in this way: (1) Tell 'em what you're gonna to tell 'em. (2) Tell 'em. (3) Tell 'em what you told 'em. That has not exactly been my own preaching style, though I admit it has a compelling logic. As I try to wrap up this book, however, I would like to try to "tell 'em what I told 'em" in the prior pages. In the chapters leading to this conclusion, the logic of my theological proposal, with a superimposed structure of prepositions (above, beneath, around, beside, etc.[3]), might be summarized as follows:

God	God who is above the "God" we have misunderstood	Above
Always	*is the underlying energy of lifegiving potential in all things.*	Beneath
Does	*God, being only what God is, but always all of what God is,*	Around
Everything	*leads us into a deeper understanding of humanity and divinity,*	Beside
Love	*teaching us to recognize that bad things will happen, and that Love is the only power we need.*	With
Can	*Even when Love cannot change our reality,*	Behind
Do	*God embraces our circumstances and walks before us into a future of hope.*	Before

Since I've begun by speaking of preaching, let me continue in that vein. An old joke among preachers asks, "How many points are there in a good sermon?" The punch line pokes fun at poor preaching: "At least one!" If this book can be taken as a sermon, a reflection of the ongoing conversation between God and one pastor trying to be attentive to his faith and his world—his faith within his world—the singular point is this: *I believe the essence of God is not power as brute force, so I accept that there are some things God simply cannot do, while I also affirm that God is real, an active energy in this world, always doing all that really matters through the power of love.*

If this is true—and it *is* true in my experience—how do we recognize that love, experience that love, and know that love? How is it, in a world that is now obsessed with proofs and facts, that we might come to really believe in something like . . . *love*? And what is it that love truly does that makes love all that really matters?

3. See an explanation of the use of "The Prepositions" in the preface.

Propositions and Prepositions

As I told you earlier in this book, I am the product of two English majors, who ground subject/verb agreement, proper punctuation, and pronoun usage into my brain. They don't teach the structure of the English language in school anymore, and I'm puzzled by how it could be so completely unimportant today when it was so critically important when my teachers were drilling the parts of speech through diagramming sentences. Do you remember diagraming sentences, all those boxes and circles and single and double underlines? In those exercises I learned to identify subjects, verbs, infinitives, gerunds, all the parts of speech, including those little, seemingly unimportant *prepositions*.

As I contemplate this God in whom I now believe, this powerful God who can't, I need to conclude by reflecting on the characteristic that must be most important if God really is Love. In that light, and based on all that my parents taught me about grammar and the Divine, I want to suggest that it might be helpful to think of this experience we name God as "prepositional." Prepositions express connectivity and relationship: *on* the table, *through* the woods, *up* the mountain, *between* two lovers, *in* my heart.

God is prepositional.

Anyone who has ever loved, or been loved, will understand that the word "love" inherently refers to an experience of relationship and connection: I fell *for* her. I'm all *about* her. I just want to be *with* her. I'm madly *in* love. So, if God = Love, and love = relationship, then, using the transitive property of mathematics, God = Relationship. In the language of this book, God is prepositional. A more common way of conceiving of the Divine may be to think of God as *propositional*, that is, related to beliefs, cognitive judgments, mental assent. As propositional, God is an idea to be comprehended or a Being to be accepted. As prepositional, God is an energy to be felt, a relationship to be experienced, not out there somewhere, but deep within.

God is not a proposition.

God is prepositional.

God is not a rule.

God is a relationship.

God is not a being.

God is a doing.

God is not a noun.

God is a verb.

God is not a thought.

God is a feeling.

God is not a concept.

God is a movement.

God is not power.

God is love.

Recently I had a conversation with a woman who knew my theological positions were decidedly different from those expounded at her conservative church. She talked about the positions she was hearing from the pulpit at her church, *propositions* about God and the world, and then she reflected on the conflict she was experiencing between what she was hearing, being asked to think and to believe, and what she was feeling within. Her *experiences* of the world through her church were not in sync "with my spirit," she said. My friend voiced concern for her friends, whose lives would not be approved by her pastor, and for the perceptions of her church, and the broader Christian church in the world due to the militant positions she was hearing. She said, "This is not sitting well with my soul. It doesn't feel like Jesus!"

I encouraged my friend to listen to her soul, because Jesus said "the [kin-dom] of God is *within* you!" (Luke 17:21 NRSV)

The Kin-dom of God is Within You

Some Pharisees once asked Jesus about the coming of the kingdom. We can assume they were interested in the return of Israel to sovereignty, self-rule, the overthrow of Roman domination, though in the evangelical worldview that is so prevalent around us that "kingdom of God" is sometimes confused with end times predictions, next life obsessions. To both his contemporaries and ours, Jesus's response was timely and timeless.

The Pharisees pondered those "signs of the times" as events for their lifetime; premillennial dispensationalists consider such signs events for the apocalypse, which they often presume will be in their lifetime. Either way, these signs might be thought of as propositions: discrete, clear, definable proofs of something big that is about to happen. Jesus had no patience for either of those eschatological visions. He said, "The kingdom of God is not coming with things that can be observed" (Luke 17:21 NRSV).

The Greek word is *parateresis*, literally "ocular evidence," and for Jesus, God's kingdom is not about ocular evidence. It's a kin-dom, not a king-dom! You're not going to see it out there, visibly, with "signs." You're not going to be able to point to it, show it to anyone else as an undeniable sign, because God's kin-dom is not a sign, an event, a happening—it's certainly not a proposition! So, if it does not come with visible evidence, God's kin-dom must not be either a new governmental sovereignty, as some disciples thought, or a literal, apocalyptic heaven, as some Evangelicals believe. According to Jesus, God's kin-dom is something altogether different.

The coming of the kin-dom is not objective. The kin-dom of God is subjective. It will not, because it cannot, be seen out there. It can only be experienced and known *within you*.

God's love is not an intervention.

God's love is an inheritance.

Interventions and Inheritances

I suppose there is a dangerous implication, for orthodox thought, that could be read in Jesus's response. Some religious movements speak not of God "out there," as a Being, separate from us in time and space, a deity on high. They speak of God as part of us, just as we are part of the Divine. For Christians raised in the Evangelicalism, which was my tradition, John Calvin's doctrine of total human depravity was too influential to ever allow such a heresy. In that Calvinistic theology God is pure good and humans are depraved creatures, rotten to the core of our hearts. God's love "saved a *wretch* like me!"[4] We and God could not be more completely separated. To say "the kin-dom of God is *within you*" would be a far too positive assessment of the human condition.

To speak of God's kin-dom within would come too dangerously close, maybe heretically close, to speaking of a spark of divinity within each of us. My mother taught me to sing, "Into my heart . . . come into my heart, Lord

---

4. This line is from John Newton's hymn, "Amazing Grace," which is sometimes regarded as *the* anthem of Christianity: "Amazing grace, how sweet the sound, that saved a wretch like me. I once was lost, but now am found. I once was blind, but now I can see." Newton, "Amazing Grace."

Jesus," but it remained crystal clear there was nothing divine about any of us, so nothing divine in us. The divinity is only in Jesus. We are not God. God is not human. And "never the twain shall meet."[5]

I have a friend whose own theological journey has led him to say, "God does not exist outside of human consciousness." Whether for him this means God is or is not *real*, I'm not sure, but my friend's challenging and unconventional implication could be implied or inferred by Jesus's words to those anxious religionists: "The [kin-dom] of God is [*inside*] you" (Luke 17:21 NRSV).

The kin-dom is not an intervention. It is an inheritance.

It is interesting to note different translations of this word "inside." The Greek preposition is *entos*, so the cognate "in" or "inside" seems clear, but the New Revised Standard has "among you." Maybe "among you" sounds less controversial, a bit safer. In my evangelical past I would have been more comfortable with a kin-dom *among us* than a kin-dom *inside me*.

Today, however, I'm drawn to the unconventional idea, even if it challenges traditional orthodoxy. Don't look for God's kin-dom, or the God of that kin-dom, somewhere out there. It's not an intervention. If you want to find God, know God, experience God, look . . . within yourself. The kin-dom, which is love, is an inheritance. Maybe it would be better to say if you want to *feel* God then be attentive to the movement of soul and spirit within, because "the [kin-dom] of God is [*inside*] you."

Pragmatic Theology and the Grandest Truth

This theology of a God who can't is pragmatic. By this I mean that in any practical way, in any way that could make a difference to us, until we have truly *experienced* something, that thing or that event is not at all real. Truth or justice or mercy or grace or sin or salvation, these can only be academic concepts unless and until we have experienced them personally. The author and philosopher Cornel West says, "Justice is what love looks like in public."[6] For West, justice is only a dry, academic idea until it comes into the marketplace to be seen, known, and experienced within.

The poet Rainer Maria Rilke says it this way:

---

5. Kipling, "Ballad of East and West," line 1.
6. Hermanns, "Justice."

I know that nothing has ever been real
without my beholding it.
All becoming has needed me.
My looking ripens things
and they come toward me, to meet and be met.[7]

Until it is real for us, to us, in us, how real could any idea really be? How could any distinct, isolated idea possibly make any difference? One might argue, academically, that absolute truths reside in some absolute nether world, whether one accepts those truths or not. Even if this were true, in actual practice, until a truth has entered into the realm of my experience, such a truth is only a proposition to be debated, discussed, and denied. In the ancient world, when it was thought that thunder and lightning showed the anger of God, for the people of that world it was *God* who made it thunder. For those people, this was reality, even though there was no factual truth to that belief. Their *belief* was all that mattered. The same is true today.

God, often conceived as the grandest of all truths, realities, and concepts, would have to be the grandest of all propositions, so, depending on your belief system, God is either the greatest of all truths, or the greatest of all falsehoods. To make of God such a proposition, so easily dismissed, too often missed, is to misunderstand God.

Though I believe God to be very real, the heart of all reality, "the energy in all things, always working for the good" (Rom 8:28), I also believe the practical reality is that *outside* of us God is just "God," a precept, an idea, a concept . . . a proposition. Only when I have known the kin-dom of God *inside* me can God change me. God can be made manifest, made truly real only through expressions of love *in us*.

The late John Claypool expresses a similar conversion of thought:

> In that moment my perceptual world was literally turned upside down, and the movement from my acquisition to awareness began. All my life . . . I had thought that in order to have worth, it is necessary to bring what is outside in, but at that moment, I say that it is the other way around: The challenge is to become aware of what is already inside by the grace of creation, and to learn to bring that fullness out through generous and sacrificial service to the whole creation.[8]

7. Rilke, *Rilke's Book of Hours*, 47.
8. Claypool, *Opening Blind Eyes*, 58.

"God is love" (1 John 4:8 NRSV), and if our world really believed that simple affirmation, this book, and thousands of others, would be unnecessary. If our ever-evolving species had internalized the inheritance granted to us from the very beginning, many wars would not have been fought, many marriages would not have failed, those families would not have been torn apart. Violence would not continue to appear to so many people as the only answer—despite thousands of years of wars and conflicts indisputably proving the contrary. Religions would not be at odds with one another, battling over their own absolute truths and territorial disputes, intellectual and geographical. We would not be afraid of the future.

If we taught our children what it really means when they say, "God is love," God could never become just an idea, a proposition, a right or wrong to be debated. God would remain only the Love that could not be denied.

The Answer That Is Not Like an Answer

The heart of my theology, a theology that began changing one day so long ago in a Systematic Theology class at Southern Seminary, is the unwavering belief that God is with us, that the kin-dom of God is in us. Through this evolved theology I have come to reaffirm a claim from the simpler faith I loved so long ago: God is the answer. The God who really is the answer, however, is not the Omnipotent Being who can do anything, anywhere, anytime. The real God is not the great fixer in the sky, the solution for all our personal problems, a divine superhero who swoops in to save the day. The real God is much more complex than that. The God who can't is much more powerful because the answer does not come as an intervention to our problems but as an inheritance of our experience.

The God who is the answer is the "God [who] always does everything Love can do." If we can learn to say that, then we can begin to *experience* God:

Above us
above the "God" we have misunderstood . . .

Beneath us
the underlying energy of life-giving potential in all things . . .

Around us
being only what God is, but always all of what God is . . .

Beside us
leading us into a deeper understanding of humanity and divinity . . .

With us
teaching us to recognize that bad things will happen—
and that Love is the only power we need . . .

Behind us
even when Love cannot change our reality . . .

Before us
embracing our circumstances
and walking before us into a future of hope.

The Final Preposition

If we can learn to say all of that, then we must learn to be comfortable saying "God is *in* us." How else could we really know Love, much less believe that God is Love, that Love is God? Once we have experienced that Love, however . . . what else is there to know?

God always does everything Love can do.

In us.

Epilog

(A Final Word, Some Final Words)

I have filled this book with words, more words in an endless stream of words about God. I have done so not because enough hasn't already been said. Enough has been said—and too much that has already been said may point in the wrong direction. If God is an idea or a Being, if the "kingdom of God" comes with some kind of ocular occurrence, then words are the point, and there's hardly enough that can be said. Explaining God, defining God, understanding God would be, precisely the point.

God.

Always.

Does.

Everything.

Love.

Can.

Do.

What I believe, however, is that an explanation of what "God" means is not the point. God is the point. The experience of God is the purpose of the words. Maybe the words just get in the way. So maybe this whole book is wrong. Maybe this exercise in breaking our theology down into definable, discrete words, words that make God easier to convey (and to control?) is the wrong way to hear the life-changing, if unorthodox, affirmation that started for me in that seminary class so many years ago.

Maybe in the final analysis the purpose of theology is not to be a tool that helps us break God down as a definable proposition or definable propositions: God. Always. Does. Everything. Love. Can. Do. Maybe the purpose of theology, like faith, is synthesis: not breaking things down, but bringing us *together*, so I can share my experience of God in us, and you can share yours.

Maybe in that sharing we will learn to say, not "God. Always. Does. Everything. Love. Can. Do," but, "God always does everything Love can do. This is what I believe because that has been my experience."

Maybe it must flow together. Maybe God is an experience, more like a sentence, flowing smoothly, connecting all the disparate pieces of my life, than God is a glossary of definable terms. Maybe all the disconnected and contradictory emotions, expressions, theologies of my life come together only, finally, when I can give up my desire for a systematic understanding: God as a proposition. Maybe God is only real when I can find God as a living experience: God in me.

In me. In you. Indeed.

May it be so.

APPENDIX A

A Prayer for Maryanne

This prayer was written January 25, 1997, at the request of members of the church I was serving. The prayer was written on the occasion of the death of a young mother, who was also a member of that congregation.

We have heard the preachers say,
   "The Lord giveth, and the Lord taketh away."

But is it possible, God
   God who made the world and said, "It is good"
   God who breathed your very own life into every living thing,
   God who came to Abraham and Sarah and offered an everlasting covenant,
   God who lifts infants to your cheek in acts of parental intimacy (Hos 11:4),
   God who in Christ claimed children and widows and prostitutes and lepers,
   God who in Christ gave your life for our very salvation . . .

Is it possible,
   good and giving and loving and yearning God
      that we have misunderstood?

      That in our attempts to explain a world beyond our comprehension,
      that in our attempts to give meaning to mean and meaningless acts,
      that in our attempts to find fault and place blame (yet to keep ourselves innocent),

that in our attempts to protect your goodness, and even your
God-ness . . .

is it possible?

In our need to write "cause and effect" over every situation,
   perhaps we need to look for you a little more in the effect (the affect).

In our desire to make you understandable, legible, calculable,
   perhaps we need to see you in the "answer" and not in the "problem."
   Is it possible?

Dare we, gracious and loving God,
   affirm this day,
      that the Lord giveth
         and the Lord giveth—even when things are taken away?

Teach us to love
   with a mind that never hesitates to ask.

Teach us to pray
   with a spirit that never ceases.

Teach us to live
   in a Grace that is sufficient
      even in our deepest need.

For Maryanne, and us this day,

"May it be so" (which means amen).

> "For in hope we were saved. Now hope that is seen is not hope. For
> who hopes for what is seen? But if we hope for what we do not see,
> we wait for it with patience. Likewise the Spirit helps us in our weak-
> ness; for we do not know how to pray as we ought, but that very Spirit
> intercedes with sighs too deep for words. And God, who searches the
> heart, knows what is the mind of the Spirit, because the Spirit inter-
> cedes for the saints according to the will of God. We know that all
> things work together for good for those who love God, who are called
> according to God's purpose. For those whom God foreknew God also
> predestined to be conformed to the image of God's Son, in order that
> he might be the firstborn within a large family. And those whom God
> predestined God also called; and those whom God called God also
> justified; and those whom God justified God also glorified."
> Rom 8:28–29

APPENDIX B

A Sermon

Are We Up to the Challenge?

1 John 5:9–13

Russ Dean, May 16, 2021

"Those who believe in the Son of God have the testimony in their hearts. . . . And this is the testimony: God gave us eternal life, and this life is in [the] Son."

We are living at a crossroads of time. What if it is one of *the* crossroads of time? All time? What if the future actually depends on how we navigate this very difficult moment? The future of our present reality? The future of all future realities? The future of the church? The future . . . of God? What if we are living through one of the crossroads of human history?

Are we up to the challenge?

I was four years old in the tumult of 1968. The Tet Offensive marked a turning point in the war in Vietnam and five hundred civilians were killed in the infamous My Lai Massacre. Martin Luther King Jr. and Robert Kennedy were assassinated within a few months of each other. There were student anti-war protests all over the world, and the Student Democratic Society and the Black Panthers were met by police violence at the

Democratic National Convention in Chicago. That iconic photo of Tommie Smith and John Carlos was taken at the Summer Olympics in Mexico City: heads bowed, black-gloved fists raised in the air, a protest against racial injustice.[1]

Historians say it was one of the nation's toughest years, and it sounds like we haven't learned much in fifty-three years. Historians also suggest the last few years rival 1968, and maybe the years surrounding the Civil War as among the most difficult the country has ever known. To racial protests and police violence and political chaos and climate crisis, add nearly six hundred thousand deaths due to the coronavirus and pandemic craziness that has accelerated the decline of church, the increase of secularism that is eclipsing God from so many lives.

Maybe this moment really is one of the crossroads . . . of all time.

Are we up to the challenge?

Robert Wright is a "New York Times" bestselling author who writes about science and politics, history and religion. His book, called *Nonzero*, is a kind of tour through human history, looking through the lens of "zero sum" game theory—which is just the idea that in every conflict there's one winner and one loser. All or nothing: "to the victor go the spoils." To the loser, nothing. That's the zero-sum game.

Wright says the history of human development is the achingly slow discovery of the nonzero-sum game. If you're old enough, you may remember Matthew Broderick's 1983 movie called *WarGames*. Control of the nuclear arsenal had been placed under the direction of a computer, accidentally accessed by a high school hacker (played by Broderick). Before recognizing what this computer is, Broderick initiates a scenario that is interpreted as a threat from the Soviet Union. The computer initiates the launch sequence for full-scale nuclear assault.

Tension mounts, because there is no way to stop the computer—but in a fit of genius, the brash high schooler asks the computer to play a series of tic-tac-toe games, which begin running at an increasingly-frantic pace. Seconds before the computer launches what would be a "mutually assured destruction" the computer recognizes the futility of tic-tac-toe—and thermonuclear war—and freezes, declaring, "WINNER: NONE."[2]

In this movie, which was far too close to reality, teaching a computer the nonzero-sum game saved the planet. There is no way to win at the game

1. "1968 Events."
2. Badham, *WarGames*.

of nuclear war. There are only losers. In *Nonzero* Robert Wright says, in essence . . . this is really all that can save us.

In the complex "game" that is life on a beautifully, intricately evolving planet, there aren't winners and losers. It's either lose-lose or win-win. We are all in this together. Life is always *Nonzero* . . . either we learn to get along, to respect one another, to love (even our enemies, as Jesus boldly suggested), either that . . . or, based on the selfish quest of the zero-sum game, our mutually assured destruction is guaranteed.

In *Nonzero* Wright admits to being agnostic, despite having been raised in a Southern Baptist church in Texas—but his skepticism offers a glimmer of hope. Near the end of the book, in the chapter entitled "You Call This a God?" Wright sounds a little like a preacher. He says,

> It may literally be within the power of our species to swing nature's moral scales . . . decisively in the direction of good; maybe it is up to us, having inherited only the most ambiguous evidence of divinity, to construct clearer evidence in the future. Maybe history is . . . not so much the product of divinity as the realization of divinity—assuming our species is up to the challenge.[3]

"Assuming our species is up to the challenge." Robert Wright, the religious skeptic acknowledges that if there is anything called divinity in this world, maybe it is up to us to construct the evidence, to "realize" God into meaningful existence in a twenty-first century world. This idea is philosophical, but there's a practical point. To paraphrase, he says some thinkers have argued that maybe God isn't responsible for history—standing on the outside, orchestrating everything, the Man Upstairs controlling all things . . . maybe there is God, but only as God comes into being through our growth and development. Just as Christians believe Jesus was the incarnation of God . . . maybe that's our calling, each of us, to actualize a little divinity into reality, to construct the evidence—by our own testimony!

If that sounds radical, unorthodox, let me say it another way, a way that makes it onto bumper stickers and into Christian contemporary music: we are God's hands and feet in the world. "You're the only Jesus some will ever see."[4] If people are going to know God, we're going to have to show God, construct the evidence, let divinity be realized through our own testimony.

If we are up to the challenge.

3. Wright, *Nonzero*, 332.
4. Will, "You're the Only Jesus."

The only thing some people know of God is what they know from the people who treat God like some jealous, tribal deity, the master of the zero-sum game. For so many people God, and faith (which is about trying to control God for our benefit), is about power. It's about conquering and winning . . . the selfishness of being right, rather than the mutuality of being in relationship . . . what's mine, even if that means you don't get any . . . the legalism of two ways: win and lose, right and wrong, black and white, orthodoxy and heresy, Christianity and everyone else. The only image of God that much of the world knows is wrapped around that kind of logic.

But this is not the God Jesus taught us. Before anyone ever heard of game theory, Jesus understood that life is nonzero. As children of God . . . when you lose, I do, too. Love your enemy . . . turn the other cheek . . . care for the least of these . . . the last will be first . . . to whom much is given, much more will be required . . . these are not the rules of a zero-sum game.

Grace, justice, the sacrificial love of Jesus . . . are not zero sum.

Jesus didn't defeat the Romans or take down the Jewish religious hierarchy. He died, in their control, with outstretched hands, the sure marks of defeat by a worldly power. Jesus gave up his life . . . to teach us a better way: love, not power.

I'm reading *Think Again: The Power of Knowing What You Don't Know*. Without speaking specifically of church at all, Adam Grant is offering us an invitation, a recipe not just to survive, but to thrive in a post-pandemic world. If we are up to the challenge.

He says most people live like preachers or prosecutors or politicians. Preachers: defensively protecting sacred ideas. Prosecutors: angrily challenging different ideas. Politicians: selfishly campaigning to sell their ideas. We need to learn to live like scientists, Grant says, questioning everything. Thinking. Testing. Rethinking . . . even our most sacredly held ideas. (Grant isn't speaking about religion but our sacredly held ideas in science, politics, sports, etc.[5]) But for the church, as history has taught us, even our actual, sacred ideas need to be questioned.

Are we willing to rethink? To rethink church? What it looks like? How it acts? What's important about church, for us and for the world? Are we bold enough to rethink faith? What it means? How it functions? Do we have enough faith to rethink . . . God? Who is God? What is God? Is God the greatest power in the world, the ultimate justification of the zero-sum game . . . the power claimed in the "divine right of kings" (justifying

5. Grant, *Think Again*.

domination and violence in the name of God) . . . the power claimed by abusive husbands and political parties and religious traditions (giving some Christians the right to claim an exclusive hold on truth). . . ? Or is God something different from that kind of power altogether?

Are we courageous enough to see the world in the eyes of the skeptics, and daringly ask: is God? Maybe Robert Wright is correct, and history is waiting on us to be the testimony of God in this world, the proof, the realization of divinity in history.

I believe the world is aching for someone to daringly construct the evidence for a nonzero sum God: a divinity who does not dominate with violence and defensively demand to be right, who does not need the imprimatur of any political party, who will not be limited by any one religious claim to truth—but a God who only claims the win-win of sacrificial love. I believe unless we learn the love of Jesus, a willingness to die for one another, to find life only by giving it away, that we are destined to our own mutually assured destruction.

Are we up to the challenge?

We may be living in one of the crossroads of all time. The future of the church . . . the future of faith . . . the future of God may quite literally be up to us to determine, by our testimony. Maybe it's time for the church to rethink it all and to give the world a nonzero-sum faith in the God of Jesus.

Are we up to the challenge?

May it be so.

Bibliography

"1968 Events." History, Jan 5, 2018. Last updated Aug 21, 2018. https://www.history.com/topics/1960s/1968-events.

Adams, Richard. "South Carolina Primary Race: Boos for Ron Paul's Foreign Policy." *The Guardian*, Jan 17, 2012. https://www.theguardian.com/world/2012/jan/17/south-carolina-primary-live-coverage.

Ahistrom, Sydney E. "Lord Acton's Famous Remark." *The New York Times*, Mar 13, 1974. https://www.nytimes.com/1974/03/13/archives/lord-actons-famous-remark.html.

Alker, Joan. "Children in the Dawn and Shadows of Life Should be a Top Priority in Budget Talks." Georgetown University McCourt School of Public Policy Center for Children and Families, July 14, 2011. https://ccf.georgetown.edu/2011/07/14/children_in_the_dawn_and_shadows_of_life_should_be_a_top_priority_in_budget_talks/.

Amanor, Andrew. "If You Understand, It Is Not God." Verbum Bible, Apr 9, 2019. https://verbumbible.com/2019/04/09/if-you-understand-it-is-not-god/.

Angier, Natalie. "Seeing the Natural World with a Physicist's Lens." *The New York Times*, Nov 1, 2010. https://www.nytimes.com/2010/11/02/science/02angier.html.

Armstrong, Karen. *The Case for God.* New York: Alfred A. Knopf, 2009.

Badham, John, dir. *WarGames.* Beverly Hills, CA: United Arts Corporation, 1983.

Ballenger, John. "God in a Song." Sermon preached at Woodbrook Baptist Church, Baltimore, on Dec 10, 2017.

Bass, Diana Butler. "The Kin-dom of God." Red Letter Christians, Dec 15, 2021. https://www.redletterchristians.org/the-kin-dom-of-god/.

The Beatles. "The Long and Winding Road." Side 2, track 3 of *Let It Be.* Written by Paul McCartney. Recorded in 1969. London: Apple and EMI, 1970.

Bell, Rob. *What We Talk about When We Talk about God.* New York: HarperOne, 2013.

Betts, Doris. "Learning to Balance." In *Of Fiction and Faith: Twelve American Writers Talk about Their Vision and Work*, by W. Dale Brown, 3–28. Grand Rapids: Eerdmans, 1997.

"Books: Scented Fountain." *Time*, orig. pub. Dec 6, 1954. https://content.time.com/time/subscriber/article/0,33009,820996-1,00.html.

Blosser, John. "For First Time, US Not a White Protestant Majority Nation." Newsmax, Mar 6, 2015. http://www.newsmax.com/Newsfront/religion-study-white-protestant/2015/03/06/id/628774/.

Bonhoeffer, Dietrich. *Letters and Papers from Prison: New Greatly Enlarged Edition.* New York: Macmillan, 1971.

Borg, Marcus J. *Days of Awe and Wonder.* San Francisco: HarperOne, 2018.

———. *The God We Never Knew: Beyond Dogmatic Religion to a More Authentic Contemporary Faith*. San Francisco: HarperOne, 1998.

Breen, Timothy. "Telos." *Telos: Dreams and Devotions for the Way* (blog). http://telosblog.com/telosalpha/.

Buechner, Frederick. *Wishful Thinking: A Theological ABC*. San Francisco: Harper & Row, 1973.

CK-12. "13.3 Power." FlexBooks CK-12. https://flexbooks.ck12.org/cbook/ck-12-middle-school-physical-science-flexbook-2.0/section/13.3/primary/lesson/power-ms-ps.

Claypool, John. *Opening Blind Eyes*. Nashville: Abingdon, 1983.

Daly, Mary. *Beyond God the Father: Toward a Philosophy of Women's Liberation*. Boston: Beacon, 2015.

Delio, Ilia. *The Unbearable Wholeness of Being: God, Evolution, and the Power of Love*. Maryknoll, NY: Orbis, 2013.

Eck, Diana. *Encountering God: A Spiritual Journey from Bozeman to Banaras*. Boston: Beacon, 1993.

Emspak, Jesse. "Speed of Light May Not Be Constant, Physicists Say." Live Science, Apr 27, 2013. https://www.livescience.com/29111-speed-of-light-not-constant.html.

"Excursus." Merriam-Webster. www.merriam-webster.com/dictionary/excursus.

Frey, William H. "The US Will Become 'Minority White' in 2045, Census Projects." Brookings, Mar 14, 2018. https://www.brookings.edu/blog/the-avenue/2018/03/14/the-us-will-become-minority-white-in-2045-census-projects/.

Gibran, Kahlil. *The Prophet*. New York, Alfred A. Knoph, 1983.

"God as Ground of Being." Religious Naturalism. https://religiousnaturalism.org/god-as-ground-of-being-paul-tillich/.

Godsey, R. Kirby. *When We Talk about God, Let's Be Honest*. Macon, GA: Mercer University Press, 2006.

Grant, Adam. *Think Again: The Power of Knowing What You Don't Know*. New York: Viking, 2021.

Griffin, Pam. "Story Behind the Song: A Man Saved by 'Ten Thousand Angels.'" The Destin Log, Mar 24, 2017. https://www.thedestinlog.com/story/lifestyle/faith/2017/03/24/story-behind-song-man-saved-by-ten-thousand-angels/21899024007/.

Hartshorne, Charles. *The Divine Relativity: A Social Conception of God*. New Haven, CT: Yale University Press, 1948.

Haught, John F. "Teilhard de Chardin: Theology for an Unfinished Universe." In *From Teilhard to Omega: Co-Creating an Unfinished Universe*, edited by Ilia Delio, 7–23. Maryknoll, NY: Orbis, 2014.

Hermanns, Kris. "Justice Is What Love Looks Like in Public." Pride Foundation, Feb 14, 2017. https://pridefoundation.org/2017/02/justice-is-what-love-looks-like-in-public/.

Holbert, John C. *The Ten Commandments: A Preaching Commentary*. Nashville: Abingdon, 2002.

"I've Been a Deep Believer My Whole Life." Humans of New York. https://www.humansofnewyork.com/post/90268158526/ive-been-a-deep-believer-my-whole-life-18-years.

Jackson, Wayne. "The Origin of Christianity." Christian Courier. https://christiancourier.com/articles/the-origin-of-christianity.

Johnson, Elizabeth A. *Ask the Beasts*. London: Bloomsbury, 2014.

King, Martin Luther, Jr. *Strength to Love*. Boston: Beacon, 1963.

Kipling, Rudyard. "The Ballad of East and West." The Kipling Society. https://www.kiplingsociety.co.uk/poem/poems_eastwest.htm.

Kittel, Gerhard, ed. *Theological Dictionary of the New Testament*. Vols. 2 and 3. Grand Rapids: Eerdmans, 1977.

Kushner, Harold. *Why Bad Things Happen to Good People*. New York: Schocken, 2001.

Lischer, Richard. *The End of Words: The Language of Reconciliation in a Culture of Violence*. Grand Rapids: Eerdmans, 2005.

Loader, William. "First Thoughts on Year C Gospel Passages from the Lectionary: Lent 3." Bill Loader. https://billloader.com/LkLent3.htm.

Lyotard, Jean-François. The Postmodern Condition. Manchester: Manchester University Press, 1984.

McCabe, Herbert. *God, Christ, and Us*. New York: Continuum, 2003.

McGill, Arthur C. *Suffering: A Test of Theological Method*. Philadelphia: Westminster, 1982.

Miles, Jack. *God: A Biography*. New York: Alfred A. Knopf, 1995.

Mitchell, Stephen, trans. *A Book of Psalms: Selected and Adapted from the Hebrew*. New York: HarperPerennial, 1993.

Mogabgab, John S. "In Whom Shall We Trust?" *Weavings: A Journal of the Christian Spiritual Life* 5.5 (1990) 2–3.

Moore, Thomas. *Meditations*. New York: HarperCollins, 1994.

"News, Views, Notes, and Quotes." Prayer and Politiks, Apr 19, 2018. https://prayerandpolitiks.org/signs-of-the-times/news-views-notes-and-quotes-54/.

Newton, John. "Amazing Grace! (How Sweet the Sound)." Hymnary, orig. pub. 1779. https://hymnary.org/text/amazing_grace_how_sweet_the_sound.

Noah, Timothy. "Bill Clinton and the Meaning of 'Is.'" Slate, Sep 13, 1998. https://slate.com/news-and-politics/1998/09/bill-clinton-and-the-meaning-of-is.html.

Norris, Kathleen. *A Vocabulary of Faith*. New York: Riverhead, 1998.

"Old Time Religion." Hymnary. https://hymnary.org/text/it_was_good_for_our_mothers.

"Omnipotent." Merriam-Webster. www.merriam-webster.com/dictionary/omnipotent.

Oord, Thomas Jay. *The Death of Omnipotence and the Birth of Amipotence*. Grasmere, ID: SacraSage, 2023.

Parsons, John J. "The Hebrew Name of God: El and the El Constructs Given in Tanakh." Hebrew for Christians. https://hebrew4christians.com/Names_of_G-d/El/el.html.

R.E.M. "It's the End of the World as We Know It (And I Feel Fine)." Side 1, track 6 of *Document*. Recorded in 1987. Nashville: Sound Emporium, 1987.

Rilke, Rainer Maria. *Rilke's Book of Hours: Love Poems to God*. New York: Riverhead, 1996.

Sacks, Jonathan. *The Great Partnership: Science, Religion, and the Search for Meaning*. New York: Schocken, 2011.

Schilling, David Russell. "Knowledge Doubling Every 12 Months, Soon to be Every 12 Hours." Industry Tap, Apr 19, 2013. http://www.industrytap.com/knowledge-doubling-every-12-months-soon-to-be-every-12-hours/3950.

Shakespeare, William. *The Tragedy of Hamlet, Prince of Denmark*. The Complete Works of William Shakespeare. http://shakespeare.mit.edu/hamlet/full.html.

Strong, James. *Strong's Exhaustive Concordance of the Bible: The Old Time Gospel Hour Edition*. Lynchburg, VA: The Old-Time Gospel Hour, n.d.

Teilhard de Chardin, Pierre. "Teilhard de Chardin Quote of the Week (May 6): Harnessing the Energies of Love." Teilhard de Chardin, May 6, 2013. https://teilhard.

com/2013/05/06/teilhard-de-chardin-quote-of-the-week-may-6-harnessing-the-energies-of-love/.

Tennyson, Alfred Lord. "Idylls of the King: The Passing of Arthur." Poetry Foundation. https://www.poetryfoundation.org/poems/45325/idylls-of-the-king-the-passing-of-arthur.

———. "In Memoriam A. H. H." Representative Poetry Online. https://rpo.library.utoronto.ca/content/memoriam-h-h-obiit-mdcccxxxiii-all-133-poems.

"Theodicy." Merriam-Webster. www.merriam-webster.com/dictionary/theodicy.

Tillich, Paul. *The Courage to Be*. New Haven: Yale University Press, 1980.

Tupper, E. Frank. A Scandalous Providence: The Jesus Story of the Compassion of God. Macon, GA: Mercer University Press, 2013.

"U.S. Public Becoming Less Religious." Pew Research Center, Nov 3, 2015. http://www.pewforum.org/2015/11/03/u-s-public-becoming-less-religious/.

Walker, Alice. *The Color Purple*. London: The Women's Press Limited, 1983.

Weatherhead, Leslie. *The Will of God*. Nashville: Abingdon, 1972.

Whitehead, Alfred North. *Adventures of Ideas*. New York: MacMillan, 1969. https://ia801509.us.archive.org/35/items/in.ernet.dli.2015.506439/2015.506439.adventures-_text.pdf.

Whitmire, Tim. "Coach: 'It's One Loss, and It Is What It Is' John Fox Won't Sugarcoat the Panthers' First Loss of the Season, But He Doesn't Expect a Collapse Like Last Season's." *Greensboro News and Record*, Oct 21, 2003. https://greensboro.com/coach-its-one-loss-and-it-is-what-it-is-john-fox-wont-sugarcoat-the/article_f9e5b8bd-dc1d-5e10-ac1c-cfc210f79bc1.html.

Will, David. "You're the Only Jesus." Davis Will's side, track 2 of *Side by Side*. Written by Gordon Jensen. Nashville: DaySpring Records, 1983.

Williams, Rowan. *Meeting God in Mark*. Louisville: Westminster John Knox, 2015.

Wright, Robert. *Nonzero: The Logic of Human Destiny*. New York: Vintage, 2001.

Yadav, Gaurav. "An Eye for an Eye Makes the Whole World Blind." *The New Indian Express*, May 1, 2022. https://www.newindianexpress.com/lifestyle/spirituality/2022/may/01/an-eye-for-an-eye-makes-the-whole-world-blind-2447604.html.

Printed in the USA
CPSIA information can be obtained
at www.ICGtesting.com
JSHW010948151123
51824JS00012B/309